REAL ESTATE & BEYOND

A comprehensive guide for
the seller
the buyer
the realtor

by

CARMELA ZITA KAPELERIS

IØWI

Real Estate & Beyond
a comprehensive guide for the seller, the buyer, the realtor
by
Carmela Zita Kapeleris

published by:
In Our Words Inc./www.inourwords.ca

cover photo of author:
Lenora Farrell

compiled and edited by:
Cheryl Antao-Xavier

cover and book design:
Shirley Aguinaldo

Library and Archives Canada Cataloguing in Publication

Kapeleris, Carmela Zita, author
    Real estate & beyond : a comprehensive guide for the seller, the buyer, the realtor / by Carmela Zita Kapeleris.

ISBN 978-1-926926-71-1 (paperback)

    1. Real estate investment--Canada. 2. House selling--Canada. 3. House buying--Canada. 4. Real estate agents--Canada. I. Title. II. Title: Real estate and beyond.

HD316.5.K36 2016   333.33'83   C2016-906415-8

DEDICATION

I dedicate this book to my children Andrea Rose and Christopher George. I am so proud of them. They will inherit this world and make it a much better place.

In loving memory of my mother Rose, in heaven with my dad by her side. Even though they went away, I know they are still with me every day.

This book is dedicated to my soulmate and all the people everywhere that I love. They say there is a reason why things happen to you in your life... Love it! Live it! and Learn from it! The universe will show you the way!

CONTENTS

"The ache for homes lives in all of us,
the safe place where we can go as we are
and not be questioned."

– *Maya Angelou*

FOREWORD
by *Louis Kapeleris*

I am so proud to be writing these words for Carmela's book, her first of many, I hope. It is a book that I know to be long overdue for her as a career professional realtor and for the industry especially. In our work together as realtors over the last 30-plus years, we have seen people struggle with the decisions that have to be made when it comes time to sell, buy or help a loved one make these tough decisions. Countless times—in fact probably more often than not—Carmela and I have gone through the motions of allaying fears, walking clients through the process, instructing, repeating many times information and procedures to closing a transaction.

Carmela has achieved great success in our profession. She is dedicated, committed and determined to provide the best possible results for her clients. Carmela works hard and endlessly striving for excellence in all that she does. She has an enduring passion to see that all involved in the industry benefit from the expertise of those who have spent many years doing this job. I am so glad to see her follow up her success with the TV show with this highly informative book. *Real Estate & Beyond*—the book and the TV talk show do precisely that— they go beyond the business of real estate to educate others, be they buyers, sellers novice or veteran realtors to understand the 'systems' as they are and how to navigate them.

We need professionals in our industry to 'give back' to the community they operate in by initiating ideas to raise the level of understanding, adherence to right principles, promote ethics and integrity in all our dealings—something which is what we have come to expect in our Canadian way of life and that Carmela has integrated into her own principles, made it her 'motto' and faithfully exercises her gift to give back to society and the people she meets everyday.

I hope you enjoy reading this book as much as I did.

INTRODUCTION

In my search for excellence as a realtor who is passionate about her work and the people she associates with and assists, I was inspired—almost impelled—to put together this handy, easy-to-follow self-help book on real estate. I have met many buyers, sellers and even realtors who are bewildered, even taken aback by the process involved in the business of real estate. In the case of clients, this 'not-knowing' is often the deterring factor for their reluctance to venture into buying their dream home or selling a house that no longer works for them. For the novice realtor, the hard realities of the business are equally daunting. Hence this book!

The rapidly accelerating pace in the real estate industry, along with the superfluity of digital technology has left many buyers, sellers and even realtors disheartened. Perhaps that is the problem. There is an overload of information, lots of it nonessential and ultimately confusing for the average person, who just wants to sell their house or buy a home. As a realtor, I often find myself demystifying the process with new clients. Again and again, over the years, I explained the right way to do things and cautioned against the wrong way, which is fraught with risks and obstacles that most often end up as the 'horror stories' of real estate deals gone horribly wrong. All of us know someone with a sad story about a property sale. Consequently, my passion for doing the job right and dedication to the real estate profession is essentially the reason why I wrote this book!

I hope you, the reader, will find the answers to the questions that have been puzzling you and holding you back. There is a wealth of information in this book. So whether you are looking to rev up your real estate business, whether you are a buyer or a seller of a property, you would do well to read through all the sections as it will help you get a better perspective on the process and a chance to look at real estate from another viewpoint. There are many good things about the thoughts I have shared in this book. I am confident that after reading it you will be ready to assume the challenges ahead.

This book is written as a step-by-step comprehensive guide through the home buying or selling process and will hopefully serve its purpose in making your own experience as simple and stress-free as possible. In these 50 chapters, you will find tried and tested guidelines, fundamentals and procedures. And for the realtor, I have included fresh ideas, helpful programs, methods and formulas to encourage sales and productivity.

A self-introduction:

I would like to give you a brief idea about myself and my career in real estate. I have 30 years' experience as a realtor, a broker and industry expert. My realtor designations include Accredited Buyer Representative, Accredited Seniors Agent, International Real Estate Specialist and Home Stager. I love my work and feel that I have reached a point where I want to give back to the profession—the industry—that has given so much to me in terms of career satisfaction. When I received the Re/max Realtor Lifetime Achievement Award in Vegas in 2010, almost seven years ago today, my life began to change. I slowly commenced to amplify and merge my skills and transition to equally becoming a marketing media expert and real estate TV host/producer, mentor and real estate facilitator. I felt a strong desire and keen aspiration to share my skills and experience with others, clients and industry insiders alike. I believe in collaboration and cooperation, we should all support one another—for together we are stronger. I am completely assured about the tips and techniques noted in this book because I've tried them all and used them to make great changes in my life and the lives of hundreds of satisfied clients.

I've watched, listened, and sometimes found out the hard way that there are ways and means to achieving the success you desire. I have had some amazing teachers. I've studied social psychology and personal development, have taken countless workshops and classes, and read every book I could get my hands on. My interest in what makes people tick extended beyond the world of real estate, and into the areas of lifestyle management and life coaching. I wanted to explore the motives behind different behaviours and understand why people do what they do. I made sure to keep an open mind with every lesson I learned, I applied to my own life first and then decided whether it felt right for me to incorporate into my beliefs. Through the years of experimenting, I have created my own version of the best of the best within this book, which I hold myself accountable for and use on a daily basis to assist my clients and ultimately the industry on the whole.

I made this book as fun and easy to digest as I could, so that you can actually **take action** and experience the results that you are truly after. For sellers, it could be getting top price for their home in the shortest possible time with the least headaches. For buyers, it could be winning their dream home in a multiple bidding war or finding that special handyman renovation. And for realtors, it may be increasing sales or being at the top of their game, offering optimal service with integrity to their clients.

How to read this book:

Finishing a book cover to cover is an amazing accomplishment, but putting the theory into action is where your life actually transforms. Life will continue to shower us with new situations and with these tools in your armed cache you will be ready to meet them head on. We could read a book about baseball all day but till we get on the field and actually practice the game, its all theory. Same goes for Real Estate! So whether you're a seller, buyer or realtor, never give up and keep trying till your dreams become your true reality.

You can choose to go through the book from the start or go directly to the section of your interest. Whatever way you choose to read, I highly recommend that you do your research and incorporate these new and powerful ideas into your life and be proactive in your decision to sell, buy or do business in real estate.

As a realtor, you will find the keys to creating meaningful conversations, powerful 'scripts' that work, and being more prepared and confident as you set out. You will learn about vision boards and action boards to help you focus and set goals and go after them.

We hope that everyone will have many light bulb moments with new insights to change your life and the way of doing business. I hope you will all use this book to take action and to continue your own growth curve by seeking and incorporating new ideas and approaches. And remember, we get out of life what we put into it! Keep learning for amazing results!

This book has been inspired by the many talented guests I have had the honour and great pleasure to meet over the years at events, workshops, speaking engagements, radio and television shows. The inspiring conversations with great minds have been such a wonderful learning experience.

I want to acknowledge all of you—teachers, friends, colleagues, clients, and participants in audiences. It was a pleasure to learn and grow with you. You enrich many lives by sharing your challenges and successes. My heartfelt thanks to hundreds of workshop participants for providing feedback, suggestions, and real life examples that formed the basis of the book.

To my colleagues and business associates for vital information in the worlds of finance, sales, designing, customer service, relationships and all home-related products.

To my editor, for wholeheartedly believing in me and cheering me on with wisdom and praise.

To my parents, for telling me, "You can do anything you set your mind to!" To my family, for their patience, understanding and encouragement as I plugged away at my laptop.

Finally, to those of you turning these pages, my heartfelt thanks for buying the book and starting your real estate journey with me.

My best,

Carmela

"Don't worry about being successful but work toward being significant and the success will naturally follow."

– Oprah Winfrey

SECTION I   THE SELLER

Chapter 1: Five simple steps to get you started

If you really think about it, you could probably find a thousand-and-one things you need to do before your home is ready for that 'For Sale' sign to be tacked on out front. I have created a simple 5-step guide to help you get started.

Step 1: Decide when to Sell

Timing can influence your home's selling price. Other factors like how quickly you need to sell, whether it's a buyers' or sellers' market; supply and demand; the state of the economy; interest rates; and a few other factors can all effect the final selling price of your home. Time of year/season also has a large bearing on the number of 'For Sale' signs going up around neighbourhoods, Spring and Fall being the busier times.

Projected sale date: _____

Step 2: Go to the Bank—Check your Mortgage—Prepare your Finances

Will the buyer "assume" your mortgage or are you "discharging" it (paying if off)? Is there a penalty fee for discharging? Is the mortgage portable (can you put it towards your new home)? If so, how much can you increase your monthly payments to cover a higher amount? What are the property taxes, insurance fees, mortgage interest, etc.? These are important questions to ask your realtor and your mortgage specialist.

Bank appointment: _____

Step 3: Find a Real Estate Agent who is right for you

The realtor who helped you buy your home is a good place to start. Or look for names on "For Sale" signs in your neighbourhood. Your realtor should be someone who is experienced, works full-time in the profession, and is a 'specialist' in your area (knows the merits/demerits of the location). Ask your friends and family for referrals. Make sure to interview two or three realtor candidates and choose the one you feel most confident and comfortable with.

Realtor: _____

Realtor: _____

Step 4: Sign a Listing Agreement with a realtor/their brokerage to market and sell your home

Determine your home's asking price. The right asking price will attract buyers and pay you a maximum return. Setting the price too low means you could miss out on thousands of dollars. Setting the price too high will discourage potential buyers. Your realtor will check the prices of homes in your area through a real estate listing service to determine the properties that have sold, are up for sale, as well as those that did not sell. List two evaluations, high and low, for an average list price.

Price range: _____

Price range: _____

= average price range: _____

Step 5: Prepare your home for sale

See your home through a buyer's eyes: get rid of the clutter; do a thorough clean up indoors and in the yard; do all minor repairs and renovations as needed. I deal with this topic in Chapter 2: Make a 'prep' plan and To-Do list. This is an important step in house sales because the condition of your home will determine your asking price. Buyers usually look for a move-in ready house. However, it helps to weigh the cost of all your improvements versus the potential financial return. If you do not want to undertake expensive updates like replacing your roof or kitchen appliances, etc. then your realtor can negotiate that into the asking price.

Repair:	Cost:
Reno:	Cost:
Repair:	Cost:
Reno:	Cost:
Total Approx. Cost:	

Chapter 2: Make a 'prep' plan and To-Do list

Ever put your home up for sale? If your answer is 'yes,' chances are you were overwhelmed with other people's horror stories of how a sale could go wrong. Really wrong. But then if you do your research—and make a plan and a To-Do list, you have better chances of avoiding becoming the latest 'horror story.'

I've been in the business of real estate for the last 30 years. I've lost count of the number of homes I've bought and sold for my clients. I know that selling your home is probably one of the toughest decisions you'll have to make. Emotions run high and thoughts of moving and where to begin that humungous task of packing can be extremely stressful. In this chapter, I hope to give homeowners a few simple but important tips on how to prepare your home for sale. I have added check lists wherever I felt it would be helpful. Hopefully these tips will organize your thoughts around concrete steps that need to be taken to ease the stress of selling.

Hence, I will begin from where you have already *made* the decision to sell and are asking yourself NOW WHAT?? Do I sell it myself, through a friend or call in a realtor? Do I look for a home first or do I sell this first and then look for a new house? (See *Chapter 3: Selling your home without an agent; Chapter 5: Should you list your home with a friend?*)

Realtor: do I really need one? Buy or sell first?

The most common way to sell a house in Canada is to list the sale with a realtor. An average of 90% of homeowners sell through real estate agents. How you sell your house is a vast topic in itself and therefore I deal with it in a separate chapter. I also deal with the issue of buying or selling first in another chapter.

Whatever you decide, there are a few steps you need to take on your own before the 'for sale' sign goes up.

Step 1: Know your house

Organize all the paperwork that deals with your house into one folder. If you don't already have a file with your house papers, then you need to create one. Put all house related papers into the file, e.g. the deeds to the property, the layout plan, your property tax sheet, survey, mortgage agreement/payment receipts, lines of credit (liens, etc.), renovations, repairs, installation and maintenance papers.

Use the form in Table I to list details about your house. Fill out the form and keep a print out in your file.

Table I gives you a pretty good idea of your house/property and is information in a nutshell, very handy for when your realtor comes in to assess your home or to be organized.

Note: In the chapter on 'Staging your home,' I go into more detail about the 'look' you need to create for your home before you list it on the market.

TABLE I: *Details of house*

Address:		
What year built:		Age of furnace:
Type of home:		Square footage:
#Bedrooms:		#Bathrooms:
#Kitchen:	Fireplace:	Basement: Finished
Separate Entrance:	Garage:	Parking spaces:
Age of roof:	Age of windows:	
Extras included:		
Upgrades:		
Aluminum Wiring ☐	Knob/tube ☐	
Fuse box ☐		Electrical panel ☐
Mailbox location:		

Step 2: Check on the condition of your house

The condition of your house, inside and out, reflects on its value. Good maintenance and upkeep are strong selling features for any property, but particularly for older homes. Consequently, as a homeowner you may overlook or not be aware of certain factors that negatively impact the sale of your house. I've prepared a checklist in Table II which will be useful in assessing the condition of your home. Check off each of the points/areas that are in good condition and mark a cross where something needs to be fixed or changed or updated in the corresponding To-Do list.

Check off each of the items in **Table II** (on next page) that are in good condition (✓) or list the work to be done in the other column. After doing this you will end up with a to-do list of any work needed.

Read 'Buyer Beware Checklist' in Section II for more 'cures' and quick fixes for common maintenance issues in your home. With a little effort, you could take these tasks off your future home owner's list and make your property show better and increase its price value.

Remember kitchens and bathrooms sell homes! Wood floors, granite countertops are in demand. Windows, doors, bannisters, upholstery, everything should be clean, dusted, with no visible stains. These rooms should be updated, stage and decorated. (See Chapter 6: Setting the stage for the show and Chapter 7: Renovations that give the highest return)

Each of the points above add value to your home if repairs are done and maintenance is up to date. They may seem like routine, common sense chores, but when handled simultaneously on a To-Do list, it seems less of a hassle, and lessens the chances of something important being left out. Conversely, poor maintenance gives a poor first impression to prospective home buyers and negatively effects the sale. When it comes to buying a home, buyers want to fulfill their wish list, not have to create a to-do list! They are willing to pay more for a home that has been updated and is well-maintained.

Table II

The table is filled in with **suggestions***. Your home will have different needs and hence a different To-Do list.*

House exterior:	To-Do List	Timeline	Budget
Roof	Needs replacement	Immediate	best quote
Furnace			
Paintwork	Paint garage door		DIY
Foundation			
Deck/patio	Paint deck		
Fence			
Landscaping			
Driveway			
Walkway/steps			
Garage			
Porch/ enclosure			
All Rooms:	**To-Do List**	**Timeline**	**Budget**
Water damage	Main shower		
Light fixtures			
Smoke alarms/ carbon mono		Change all alarms immediately	$750
Doors / windows		Wash/repaint	DIY
Flooring	Carpets need pro cleaning		
Kitchen	Reno needed		Get 2-3 quotes
Bathroom 1			
Bathroom 2			
Bathroom (guest)	Remove wallpaper/paint		
Bedroom 3			
Family room			
Basement	Leaks, mould, mildew	Call plumber Monday	

Chapter 3: Selling your home without an agent

While many homeowners sell their house with the assistance of a realtor, some prefer to handle it themselves. Selling your home without an agent can be a lengthy, complex process. The biggest downside is the demand on your time, and the legal and financial risks from inexperience.

Remember, verbal agreements cannot be enforced. Put every aspect of your contract in writing and make sure that everyone involved signs the agreement. Be aware of any conditions the buyer has added to their offer. Preparing the proper documents, legal forms, disclosures, waivers, amendments etc. are your responsibility. Even the smallest mistake can mean serious trouble.

Your safety comes first. The majority of lookers are honest people and quite possibly serious home buyers. However, security measures are necessary for the possibility that one of the visitors could see your home as an opportunity for crime. So my advice is: Make all your showings by appointment only. Always get a name and number and call back to verify the caller. In some cases, ask for ID or driver's license before you let a stranger in to view your home.

Place all valuables out of sight. Hide **all** prescription drugs. Eliminate displays of personal information. Accompany them at all times. Beware of casual questions like "Do you have a security system?" "Why aren't you using a realtor? Is there something wrong with the property?" and "Since you aren't using an agent, can we take their fee right off the top?"

'For Sale By Owner' homes typically attract bargain hunters who often expect you to lower your price since they, too, are looking to save money on the real estate fees. These buyers will often deduct the fees from your asking price and then start low ball negotiation with you from there.

For many unrepresented sellers, the financial savings are disappointing. Payment of fees to outside attorneys, consultants, inspectors, appraisers, and loan officers, marketing, advertising... not to mention the time wasted in sourcing out and negotiating with each of these professionals—can have owners asking themselves: would I have been better off paying the agent fee which would have included many of these charges up front? The benefit of a professional realtor is that you can leave it in their hands to use all of their resources, knowledge, skills and expertise to get the best deal for you, i.e. maximum exposure and the highest price.

By far, the greatest advantage of all is having a realtor on your side of the negotiation procedure. Having a real estate agent that is a good negotiator can possibly cover their entire commission by not leaving money on the table when it comes to settling on a final price. It is ultimately your decision!

Chapter 4: Choosing an agent—what to ask

What questions should you ask when hiring a real estate agent? When it comes time to listing a home, most sellers generally have two questions for their realtor: How much will you get for the property and what will the commission be?

Few sellers take time to ask additional questions. Many hire an agent on appearance and gut feeling. But selling a home is a very big and important transaction. Sellers should ideally interview 2-3 realtors and ask a wide range of questions to find out why an agent is better than the others before they make a decision. Which agent is the seller most comfortable with in terms of trust, attitude, professionalism, empathy to their situation and impeccable service.

As a **seller**, you will need to know some key information about each agent and their modus operandi. Here are some questions that you could use when interviewing. Note the agent's answers down in a notebook:

- *Are you a full-time or part-time realtor?*
- *How long have you been working in my neighbourhood?*
- *How many homes have you listed in the past six months?*
- *What specific steps will you take to sell my home?*

Ideally, a realtor should be working full-time, with at least 2 to 5 years' experience, preferably in your neighbourhood. A part time agent may not be able to deal with the complexity of a fast paced changing market and may not be available when you need them. When you select an experienced realtor, you will be getting a track record, a roster of contacts for any services you need, and a host of creative, time-tested ideas for marketing your home.

Following are questions to ask an agent you are thinking of signing up with. Don't forget to note down each agent's answers in a notebook:

- *How will you keep me informed?* Be sure to tell your agent how you would like to receive regular communication, whether weekly, daily, text, email, phone or meet in person. You need to work as a team with your agent and you deserve all the time and attention you want and need.

- *What is involved in the listing agreement?* Before you sign, make sure your agent explains the process and that you understand every detail of the contract. This is a very important step.

- *How did you arrive at that price for my home?*

- *How long will it take to sell my home?*

- *Ask how close is their list-to-selling ratio.* A competent listing agent should have a track record for negotiating sale prices that are close to list prices. As well as being able to sell houses in record time.

- *What is your best marketing plan or strategy for my needs?*

- *Where and how often do you advertise?* Will you show me a sample flyer? How do you market online?

- *What are the top three things that separate you from your competition?* A good agent won't hesitate to answer this question and tell you why she is best suited for the job. Most consumers say they are looking for agents who say they are: Honest and trustworthy, assertive, excellent negotiators, available by phone or e-mail, good communicators, friendly, analytical, able to guide and advise under trying circumstances and so on.

- *What haven't I asked you that I need to know?* Pay close attention to how the real estate agent answers this question because there is often something else you may need to know. She should know how to listen and how to counsel you, to make sure you feel comfortable and secure with her knowledge and experience.

As a **buyer**, the above questions are still appropriate for picking a realtor you are comfortable with. Other questions to ask—from the buyer's perspective—are:

- *How will you search for my new home?*

- *How many homes will I see and how often?*

- *Will I be competing against other buyers?*

- *How do you handle multiple offers?*

- *Do you present offers yourself?*

Asking questions helps you gain knowledge, keeps you well informed and comfortable that you have made the right choice when it comes to someone keenly involved in one of the biggest financial decisions of your life.

Tip: Check *Chapter 34: Tasks a realtor does for you.*

Chapter 5: Should you list your home with a friend?

There are many mistakes a person can make when deciding to sell a home. One of the most serious is listing your home with a realtor just because that realtor is your friend.

The problem with having a "friend" represent you is twofold:

Is he/she the **best** agent that you can find? In other words: If this person were not your friend would you still hire him/her?

The second issue is more personal: Will your relationship with this "friend" change the way that you approach your sale? Will you be as demanding or have the same level of expectations of your "friend" as you would of an agent you have only a business relationship with?

I strongly encourage you to interview your "friend" as objectively as possible and compare his/her experience and communication skills with that of other agents. Your home is your largest investment; it pays to do your homework. The traits to look for in an agent are:

- *Confidentiality:* Will your friend keep your information confidential from your mutual friends?

- *Professionalism:* How does your friend conduct business?

- *Is this friend a realtor full time?* What is their education, experience and results record?

- *How will you and the agent friend handle a situation in the event that there is a dispute?* You should never feel obligated to use a friend. You should hire the agent you think will do the best job and get you the highest net proceeds for your home. Realtors mostly practice in their area of expertise. Is your home located in your friend's area of expertise? If not, then ask her to refer you to another agent. That way you would still be supporting her business as well.

  Most people think it is not a good idea to hire anybody who has a personal interest in the property, whether it is a friend or an acquaintance or especially a neighbour. A neighbour is the worst because they may want to pick who lives next door to them.

You need to go with somebody who is neutral and objective and professional.

I hear people say that it can be much tougher working with a family member or close friend. At times, the sense of urgency is not there and emotions can sometimes really get in the way of things.

You should also never make the mistake of listing with a part time agent. Selling a home is too complicated and too important to entrust to a part time agent or friend, who by not knowing the pitfalls and complications of the business could embroil you in a lawsuit. Remember this is a business decision about your finances. Choose wisely.

"I believe that every right implies a responsibility; every opportunity, an obligation; every possession, a duty."

– John D. Rockefeller, Jr

Chapter 6: Setting the stage for the show

Your home reflects *you* and *your* taste in colours and furnishings. Yet when buyers come to view a property, they like to see themselves in the house. They like to imagine their own furniture and pictures on the walls. You want them to say "I can see myself living here."

You can do this most effectively by moving yourself out of the house before you put it up for sale. By this I mean de-personalize living spaces by taking down personal pictures, decoration items and other visual 'clutter.' In real estate lingo, this process is called 'home staging.'

Home staging can determine how fast a home sells. Your Realtor may be able to recommend a professional Home Stager who, for a fee, will go through your home room by room and help you with a layout plan. Clients are often too close to their 'stuff' to realize what aids or hinders the flow of movement through the living areas.

Need convincing that home staging is important? Check out these stats:

- *Faster sales time:* 93% of staged homes sell on average in less than two weeks

- *Higher sales price:* Staged homes sell for an average of 7% more money than unstaged homes, which means an extra $21,000 on the purchase price of a $300,000 home!

- *Staged homes look better in photos online:* Nearly 98% of Buyers 'shop' online before ever contacting a realtor. It's the first step in creating buyer interest!

- *Buyers and home inspectors view the home as well-cared for.*

- *Buyers are better able to see themselves and their future home in a minimalist staged home.*

The first step in home staging is to **declutter, declutter, declutter!** I can't say it strongly enough. The idea behind doing this is to allow rooms to show themselves rather than showcase your stuff. Remove knickknacks, wall and table décor, books, doilies, small appliances, etc. etc.—junk it, donate it, pack it up, give it to a friend...but get all table and counter surfaces, walls and mantels cleared of all but one or two appropriate items at the most. Remove pet litter boxes (and any lingering odours). Pack away toys and limit kid activity evidence to a tidy, minimalist designated area.

Small rooms look larger when there is sparse furniture. If you have large or oversized pieces of furniture that you want to keep, think about renting temporary storage space till you sell and move. Arrange smaller pieces in appealing vignette groupings of 1-3-5's. These groupings show the rooms potential. Try not to leave rooms vacant. If you have an extra bedroom, set up a desk and chair there and list it as a guest room/office.

Kitchens and bathrooms sell houses. So make sure yours are sparkling clean and updated where necessary. Breathe new life into your kitchen and bathroom cabinets with new paint and hardware. You can replace just the doors if the insides of the cabinets are in good condition and are of standard measurements. Replace countertops and vanities if needed. With renovations you need to keep an eye on your budget. Repairs and renovations add considerably to the buyer appeal, but can run into thousands. You may not be able to recover the costs in the asking price for your house.

Light fixtures can be a major feature in a room. Refreshing fixtures with metallic paint or putting in new shades can change the look. Use slipcovers over worn upholstered sofas and chairs. Remove tablecloths and polish furniture. Remove heavy window coverings and keep window treatments light and bright. Bedrooms can be beautifully 'staged' with new bed-in-a-bag coverings.

Paint can transform your home giving it a fresh look. Muted colours form a neutral background that the buyer can envision livened up to their individual tastes. That is why it pays to set your home in neutral colours for a more generic look.

Check plumbing through the house. Fix leaky faucets. Re-caulk tubs, showers and sinks. Bleach grout. Remove used towels and mats in the bathroom and kitchen and 'stage' with new ones, or else leave out. Tidy linen cupboards. Replace worn rugs and broadloom. Broken tilework and wood flooring are awkward as they are a major renovation expense. Again it is usually worth the money as you can add it to the listing price.

Read *Buyer Beware Checklist* in Section II to get an idea of quick fixes for common problems that could give a bad impression to prospective buyers.

Finally, put out a vase of fresh flowers out or a basket of fresh fruit. An old realtor's trick used to be baking a cake, so the house would welcome buyers with the homely aroma of baking. Nowadays, room fresheners come in many varieties. Go for a subtle fragrance of freshness. Treat every 'showing' with the respect it deserves—keep your house clean and welcoming.

Chapter 7: Renovations that give the highest return

The best renovations are the ones that are done in a timely manner. Don't wait to sell your home before you enjoy that updated kitchen or luxurious bathroom. You deserve to live well. You deserve to be surrounded by beauty, comfort and functionality—within your budget, of course—but nonetheless important to you and your family's wellbeing.

I see so many clients agreeing to paint, reupholster, re-floor and fix or replace broken and shabby 'things' in their home that if done through the years they were living in the house would have made life more enjoyable and less stressful.

Here are some tips on renovations that are commonly done when putting a home up for sale. If you see any of these as a do-now project, get a quote on costs, save the money, and do it. It will raise the value of your home when you do sell it.

- *Kitchen Renovations:* The kitchen is the center, the heart of the home. Because of this common perception, updates in this room pay off in resale value. According to home reno experts, you can expect to recoup 60%-120% of your investment on a remodeled kitchen. Update old appliances with stainless steel and/or energy-efficient models, which are better for the environment. Eco-friendly options continue the savings for potential buyers, who find this an important factor when shopping for a new home. The kitchen is one of the best renovations for resale value.

  Paint goes a long way. Best, easiest and cheapest way to get a return on your investment is to invest in painting the whole house neutral designer colours. You might want to consider using low-VOC paint; this makes your kitchen eco-friendlier, and helps your family avoid breathing in dangerous chemicals, like benzene, that emit from regular fresh paint.

- *Bathroom renovations or additions:* Bathrooms are a very important reno to undertake to bump up resale value. An average bathroom remodel costs around $10,500 while an upscale remodel is going to run you anywhere from a hefty $26,000 upwards, but this reno will pay off.

  If your home only has one bathroom, it makes sense to add another one and recoup a large chunk of your investment. You can recoup 80%-130% of whatever you spend on reno or by adding a bathroom.

Like any project, the cost of adding a bathroom depends largely on the types of additions and accessories you want to use. You can save money and find great prices on tubs, doors, toilets, and fixtures by frequently checking home reno centers.

- *Granite countertops:* A popular trend is to splurge on granite countertops. Because the bathroom counter is so small, the investment is often fairly low compared to what you'd spend on kitchen counters, for example.

  Neutral colors like tan, brown, and light beige are more popular. To save on the cost of granite countertops is to buy a slab containing slight imperfections located near the sink or faucets where they are not visible.

- *Renovations to finish the basement:* Basements frequently work well as second living rooms or game rooms. Many people also turn this space into a small apartment for an aging relative or tenant and therefore save or earn rental income.

  Although you can recoup some of your investment, anywhere from 50%-83%, this project's costs can quickly spin wildly out of control. According to Remodeling Magazine, an average basement remodel, with the addition of a wet bar, can cost upwards of $64,000. This can end up being an incredibly expensive project and may backfire if done for resale value; because buyers may not like the way you've renovated or would prefer to have an in-law apartment instead. Homeowners and contractors can run into unexpected problems too with basement renovations. You can be taking a chance on the use of a basement reno.

  A solution to this issue would be to do a basic reno, repaint and declutter, to create a space that can be used for whatever purpose a buyer sees fit. You could list it as a multi-purpose room. Everybody could use a multi-purpose room, right?

- *Energy-efficient windows. Good renovation investment:* Old, drafty single-pane windows are a major turn off. Energy efficient windows can save you $500 a year in heating and cooling. According to reno experts, you can expect to recoup 60%-90% of your costs when you invest in energy-efficient windows. You can also receive a green energy tax credit of 10% for this upgrade, as long as you install Energy Star-rated windows.

- *Deck addition:* Good renovation for resale value: Adding a deck increases the value of your home. If you make your deck and your backyard more appealing, your house will be more appealing to prospective buyers when you decide to sell. Homeowners recoup on average 65%-90% of their investment by adding a deck to their property.

Decks can cost anywhere from $1,200 to $10,000, or more. Again, it all depends on the size, design and materials used. As you might guess, you can save a huge amount of the cost, usually about half, by doing the work yourself.

To sum up, renovations are a cost-effective option whether you are selling immediately or just updating a room that doesn't function well any more. It adds resale value to your home and makes your life better organized, more efficient and beautiful.

Before

After

Photos courtesy Carol D'Avolio, Black Diamond Home Staging and Redesign

Chapter 8: Feng Shui—adding Qi value to your home

What is feng shui staging and how does it work? Feng shui plays an important part when it comes to staging and selling your home. In the real estate business, it has become a verb, so that many people "feng shui" their homes to create a feeling of harmony, relaxation and abundance. It is considered beneficial to assess a home, workplace or any environment to allow for optimal Qi (pronounced "chee"), which is the personal flow of energy.

With the growing number of foreign buyers purchasing property, feng shui principles are a common requirement when viewing a property to purchase. For the seller, this means that you can attract greater interest from serious buyers with the potential of generating multiple offers on your home. Adding feng shui features to your property listing is a definite plus point.

In many cases, common staging decisions are right in line with those of feng shui principles: for example getting rid of clutter, removing personal items, and creating a nice flow through the space. It may look as though the two approaches are in fact the same but they are not. Feng shui takes many factors into consideration that are not strictly required or even considered in home staging. However, applying feng shui ideas to your home staging can only benefit the sale of your home.

It is widely believed that if a house does not sell, something may be wrong with the Qi (flow) of the house. Whatever the reason for the house sale being "stuck," it could be helpful to employ some feng shui principles to open up the home to positive Qi.

Feng shui tip: Feng shui is a living skill. There is an art to it. It is scientific, it is mathematical and at times it is logical—with an element of magic!

Here are some easy to apply feng shui tips that might improve the flow of energy in your home. If you are a buyer, keep these points in mind when looking at properties. If you are a realtor, train your eye to spot the Qi-busters and switch the energy losers around to facilitate positive Qi.

- Properties that are opposite graveyards, hospitals, churches, police and fire stations are considered to carry heavy energy, sorrow and pain, which upset or radiate the pattern and flow of Qi. There is not much you can do about the area you are already located in, except to incorporate many feng shui principles into the exterior of the property to hopefully counteract the 'negativity.'

- Is your house on a "T" street? This is the case when the street ends directly in front of the house. Negative energy is created. This is considered bad Qi. You can counteract this situation by putting a large red potted plant on the porch near the front door.

- Is there clutter or high obstacles in front of the home. Is there no path to the front door? The main entry point of the home should have a cleared path leading to it. A black doormat at the front entrance will create good Qi.

- Is your front door in direct alignment with the back door? Good feng shui energy coming through the main door will easily escape through the back door without having a chance to circulate and nourish your home. To prevent this, follow the next tip.

- If you have a big window opposite the front door, energy can fly right out the window. It is advisable in such cases to use sheers or blinds. Or put something in front of the window/door, like a pretty reflective bowl or hanging crystal in the window to redirect the energy.

- Does the interior staircase face the front door—this allows Qi to negatively escape out the front door. A water feature in the foyer such as an aquarium or a fountain will create good Qi.

- Exposed beams create stress and tension. Sleeping under an exposed beam is especially bad and can lead to headaches, deceit and bad luck.

- In feng shui, the kitchen is considered the heart of the home that nourishes and sustains life. A kitchen in the center of the house is an ideal, positive location. It is 'good' to put away anything with sharp edges.

- An awkward seating plan in the living room that is not conducive to conversation is a big feng shui no-no. You want an intimate arrangement that invites people in to the room. Use the wall farthest from the entry—with a clear view of the door to arrange your seating area. Leave a few inches of breathing room between the sofas and the wall.

- The bathroom and toilet should not be visible from the front door. Doors to the bathrooms should always be kept closed. Try to create a feng shui spa in your bathroom with candles, lights, flowers, music for the ultimate Qi.

- Greenery, like plants, nurtures good energy and keeps it from leaving the home.

- Dried flowers are extremely bad feng shui. Silk flowers are acceptable, but live flowers are the best. Accessories such as picture frames, pillows, candles should be arranged in pairs.

- Mirrors can do all kinds of tricks in feng shui like recirculate energy and enhance natural light. They draw attention to what they reflect. For example, a fireplace sends energy out of a home, whereas a mirror above the mantel bounces energy back in.

- In the bedroom the head of the bed should be against the wall farthest from the door but not directly across from it. A sidewall is okay as long as you have a clear view of the door.

- Painting your home the feng shui way means that colour choice is important and creates different energies and moods within a room or house in general.

When applied in tandem, feng shui and home staging ideas benefit and compliment one another to achieve highly beneficial results in terms of upping the value of your home.

Feng shui tip: Clutter is everything unfinished, unused, unresolved or disorganized. When you clear your clutter you create space for new things and your energy and creativity will increase.

Feng shui colours

Feng shui colours are extremely powerful and can literally transform a room instantly. Feng shui colours represent different moods, flow and energy and of being one with nature. They bring about many characteristics that increase social and personal wellbeing, health, wisdom, abundance and prosperity.

Orange is very stimulating, active, cheerful and sociable. It is less arousing than red and more pleasantly stimulating. It is one of the best feng shui colours for the kitchen, dining room, and living room. If used in the bedroom, make sure it is an earthy orange. It increases oxygen intake to your brain and even makes you more sociable.

Purple represents nobility, abundance, and dignity. It is very soothing and calming and is often related to intuition and spirituality. You may use lighter purples like lavender and violet to help create a very romantic feng shui bedroom.

Grey is neutral, calm, quiet, and lacks energy. The psychological effects of grey can also be boring, conservative, indecisive and draining to the physical body. Grey is best used as an accessory colour.

Brown is stable, supportive, reliable, motherly, comfortable, and inexpensive. Like earth, brown is very grounding. Use brown in your bedroom or living room.

Red is passionate, stimulating, exciting, powerful, and expanding. The fire element is great for transformation in richness, luxury, love and romance. Red can be used in the kitchen, dining room, and living room. Earthy reds are appropriate for the bedrooms. Red is the most dominant and dynamic of colours.

Yellow is very happy, uplifting and warm. It is a wonderful colour for the kitchen, dining room, and living room because yellow draws people out and makes them more talkative. It helps to focus one's attention and stimulate the intellect. Yellow also encourages hope and optimism.

Green is very calming, balancing, healing, relaxing, and tranquil. It is the most restful colour on the eye. Greens are particularly beneficial in a bathroom because it promotes purification and a sense of freshness. Green also brings about vitality, peacefulness, life, and new beginnings.

Blue characterizes dependability, trustworthiness, and security. It can also be associated with introspection, mysteriousness and stillness. Blue represents the water element, clarity, healing, soothing. Like green, blue is one of the best feng shui colours used in the bathroom.

Black signifies sophistication, power, elegance, and modernity. It is also introspective and mysterious. It is best to use black as an accessory colour.

White represents clarity, innocence, cleanliness, spirituality, purity, hope, expansiveness and openness. White is a symbol of purity and cleanliness, so it is a fantastic colour to use in the bathroom or to accessorize.

Pink is sedating and calming. It can be a pure and innocent colour, and in turn very positive. It also symbolizes love and romance. Use the colour pink in your feng shui bedroom.

Chapter 9: Pricing your home for success

While your house is your 'Home Sweet Home,' it is important to put feelings aside and be as objective as possible when it comes to pricing it for sale. There are several factors that come into play when putting a price on your home. Here are a few of those factors you should consider carefully.

Time of year

Spring is considered the best season to sell a home since families are trying to move and settle in before the start of the next school year. The Spring season can start as early as February with Buyers opting from 3- to 6-month closing dates. Fall is a close second, since it comes right after the quiet days of summer when most people are away on vacation. Winter is the slower season, because of the snow and icy weather. At this time of the year, there are the Thanksgiving, Christmas, and New Year's holidays when people's minds are generally on socializing, rather than on buying or selling a home.

Interest rates

If interest rates are reasonable, it seems everyone is in the market to buy a home. But, if interest rates start to climb, many buyers may not qualify to buy a home or upgrade to a larger house. Pricing in this case could be more flexible.

Inventory

Supply and demand is what drives up costs. It is generally a good idea to take advantage of what is termed 'pent-up demand,' which will garner higher than usual prices on home sales. Even homes that can be difficult to sell will generally stand a better chance of selling in a pent-up demand situation. If real estate inventory is low and you—as a seller—are lucky enough to be experiencing a seller's market in your area, not only will your home be fewer days on the market, but you could also receive multiple offers, which could drive up the sale prices because of the competition.

If you're thinking of putting your home on the market, and it is anticipated that buyers are going to be competing for homes, you may be tempted to try listing it at a super high price just to see if you can get it. But don't do it. This ploy tends to backfire when you have to reduce the price and you've lost potential good offers. Don't worry about pricing the home too low because homes priced below market value will often receive multiple offers. This will drive up the selling price and precipitate a bidding war, selling for top dollar.

Some homeowners seem to want to set their list price based on what they paid for their home, the balance owing on their mortgage, or on the profit they want to make so they can move into another home. In reality, your home is worth only what the market will bear and the buyer will pay for it based on that.

If you price your home too high, some potential buyers won't want to look at it at all, while others will simply walk away without making an offer. You don't want to overprice the house because you will lose the freshness of the home's appeal after the first two or three weeks of showings, when the buyer demand and interest generally slows down.

Find the "sweet spot," also called "price banding." For example, look at the sale prices of homes in your neighbourhood. Prices tend to get bunched up as inventory moves along. Find an empty spot so your home is separated from the pack. For example, four homes are priced in the $474,000-$476,000 range and the next set of homes start around $490,000 and up. You should take advantage of the $480,000 price band.

Price your home so it will be found in real estate searches. Real estate agents usually set up automated searches for their buyers. The way it works is that the buyer tells their agent they want a three-bedroom home under $500K (or some other dollar amount), and if your home is listed at 510K or 520K, that buyer and other buyers with the same price criteria will miss your home entirely in the property searches.

While this scenario happens customarily, many keen agents will set up search parameters for their buyers to include properties listed a little bit more than their price ceiling. Buyers should be made aware of properties that could be a good match for them, even if the homes are a bit above but within reasonable range of what they want to pay. You never know if the property is going to be reduced or sometimes the buyer can offer under the list price.

If inventory increases suddenly and your home is one of 13 houses up for sale in the neighbourhood, you will have a hard time getting your price since the supply is greater now and the demand may not equal it. However, if it's a hot market and you have a home in a great neighbourhood, chances are you will get your asking price and maybe even more. Check out the neighbourhood to see if inventory is high or low. You could ask a reputable real estate agent to make the search for you.

Pricing is all about supply and demand. It's part art and part science. Some agents are much better at figuring out how to price your home than others. Experience is what matters in this matter!

Chapter 10: Seven mistakes sellers make – how to avoid them

How can you get the highest possible price for your home within a reasonable time frame AND without losing your mind?! Selling your home can be a complex, emotional experience. It's easy for home sellers to make lots of mistakes, but with a little know-how, many of these pitfalls can be avoided altogether.

Read on to find out what are the 7 most costly mistakes home sellers make and how to avoid them:

1. *Selling your home on your own:* This can cost you money. Although it may seem like you're saving the real estate fees, statistics show that homes sold without representation remain on the market longer and end up selling at a lower price than those with a realtor at the helm. The numbers don't lie.

2. *Withholding information from buyers:* Disclose everything. If you think that the buyers or their inspector won't find out about the leak in the basement or other problems, you run the risk of losing money in the negotiating period—or worse still, a lawsuit.

3. *Mispricing your home:* Pricing too high or too low can be a costly error. It's important to understand your market, to look at exactly what the recent SOLDs went for, what the comparables are currently selling for, and how long they have been on the market, to understand exactly what price tag needs to be on your home.

4. *Getting emotionally involved:* It is helpful when you sell to think of yourself as a business person rather than the home owner. Many sellers take negotiating personally and lose out as a consequence. Remember, this is a business transaction – perhaps the biggest one of your life. Try to remember how you felt when you were shopping for a home. Put your ego and emotions aside and help create a win-win situation.

5. *Refusing to tidy up before listing:* If you don't clean up the place prior to putting it on the market, you are almost guaranteed to have buyers offer less for your property. Cluttered homes take longer to sell, if not kill the deals entirely. Create an illusion of spaciousness by decluttering, top to bottom, getting rid of all the bulky stuff, accessories, etc. It costs you nothing to declutter, but brings big rewards when it's time to sell.

6. *Using lousy photos:* More than 90% of all buyers start their home search online, so it is a good idea to have your agent take professional pictures of your home. Too many for-sale homes feature amateur iPhone photos in their listings. Poor quality photos will be a poor 'showing' and you may miss out on potential buyers—and potentially thousands of dollars—if buyers pass over your listing because it didn't look attractive enough to go see.

7. *Listing a vacant house:* This is a costly mistake. Buyers sometime view a vacant house as a desperate seller situation because its empty, and does not feel lived-in. Most realtors believe that a home should be dressed or "staged for the wow factor" to retrieve the highest price possible. It would be well worth it to temporarily rent some furniture or use a local staging company to get that lived-in feel.

"Selling is not something you do to someone. It's something you do for someone."

– *Zig Ziglar*

Chapter 11: What if your home doesn't sell?

If your home has just come off the market and hasn't sold, don't be discouraged. The reason it didn't sell may have nothing to do with your home or the real estate market. In reality, your home may have been one of the more desirable properties listed for sale during that period. If your listing has expired and you still want results, before you put your home back on the market, take a step back and review your situation.

Your home is a major financial investment and your relationship with your realtor should be a full partnership where your needs and wishes should be heard. You should receive detailed and dependable feedback from the agents who have shown your home. Your agent should communicate this to you so together you can make the right decisions about what to do next. Ask yourself, did these steps take place the last time you had your home up for sale?

When interviewing agents, test and compare their knowledge and ask each to demonstrate how they will market your home to buyers. Compare, too, how much money each agent spends on advertising homes and in what media do they place the ads. Evaluate the effectiveness of one medium over the other. Remember, it's not just how much they spend, but how they spend it to achieve the best results.

Pricing is important. To help **you** establish a realistic selling price for your home, ask your agent to provide you with an up-to-date 'Market Analysis of Comparable Homes' recently SOLD and homes currently for sale. This analysis will give you an idea of how long the homes were listed, an average selling time and a review of the homes whose listings expired. You will then have a better idea of what issues are at play. This information will help you establish the right price with the right realtor.

Make your house easy to show. Consider installing a lock box. Allow showing times that are convenient to buyers. To get the best results you need to team up with your agent to develop a powerful marketing plan that exposes your property to the widest possible pool of prospective buyers.

The relationship between you and your agent can make the difference between selling your home fast, or not selling it at all.

Chapter 12: The 'For Sale' Sign — a few pointers

A 'For Sale' sign is free marketing. Hardly a day goes by that I don't receive a call from an interested buyer who saw one of my 'for sale' signs. In a hot sellers' market, you'll hear of buyers slamming on the brakes as they drive by a sign. Neighbours see it and recommend the property to family and friends. There are other benefits and drawbacks to putting up a sign. Here are a few pointers to keep in mind when considering this selling option.

Buyers check out home sale advertisements and sometimes feel the urge to go check out the property in daylight. The ad doesn't always list a house number, so if the street or neighbourhood has houses with similar features, a 'for sale' sign out front will indicate the house in the ad. If they like the outside, they may want to see the inside. If they don't see a For Sale sign, they will think it's not available.

For sale signs these days come with a QR code, which is a link to a specific web page. Interested parties walking by can scan the code with their smartphones and instantly have access to your property brochure and relevant sale details, videos of the property and its various features. They will also find the number to call to make an appointment to view the property. By not placing a For Sale sign, you may be reducing your home's exposure and losing out on potential viewers.

If you are concerned about people turning up on your doorstep wanting to see your home, ensure that your For Sale sign stipulates viewing by appointments only. If you are concerned about the length of time the sign has to stay up, don't be. If the property is marketed correctly, chances are you will be sticking a SOLD banner on it in no time.

That said, if you want to keep your property sale secret for whatever reason, then not having a sign out front is one way to achieve that.

Regarding the sign itself—be professional and clear in your message. Never be misleading with information. If you have an agent, they will screen the calls for you. If you are selling privately, you may want to be discreet about giving out your private home number or cell phone where the chance of it being picked up by telemarketers or insincere buyers and trolling agents is quite likely.

Take a look at For Sale signs wherever you see them and decide what you like. Again, if you are working with a realtor, they will guide you on signs that are tried and tested in their experience. Good luck with your sale!

Chapter 13: Open houses really do work!

If you're selling a home, you might be asking "Should I have an open house or not?" "To do or not to do... that is the question!" This topic can spark quite a debate among realtors and sellers alike. There are agents including myself who swear it's critical to have open houses and have sold many homes through marketing and holding open houses! But then there are agents who never hold open houses and others who will have them periodically. In most cases the agent is just lazy and may not want to work on weekends. In my opinion, it's always better to have an open house than not even bother.

Truth be told, there are some sellers who will insist that having open houses are an important step to selling their homes. But then again, there are others who will want nothing to do with open houses, and some sellers will be on the fence. Ultimately it is your home, so the decision is yours!

So if you are selling and you are unsure about open houses, like any decision, everything has two sides. In this case, the positives always outweigh the negatives when your selling and trying to attract buyers to your home.

Yes, it is true that the noisy neighbours always come through first, but that's not a bad thing. Although they do like to compare homes and look at your decor, in actuality they may have a relative, friend or someone from work who wants to move into the area. And what better person to spread the word than your neighbour who loves the area and has a home just like yours! They are your best source of advertising!

One of the most important things for a realtor selling a home is making sure their clients home is getting a ton of exposure. Without maximum exposure and a strong marketing system, the chances of a home selling are greatly reduced. Open houses can give additional exposure to a seller's home. Whether it's through street signs, newspaper ads, or internet ads that promote the open house—it all leads to additional exposure.

For agents and sellers who are expecting multiple offers on a home "You have to have the open house to get the people in there!" Otherwise the home may end up selling too quickly without getting the maximum exposure. It always makes sense to schedule an open house and to hold back offers or only accept offers until after that date.

Keeping the home secure during the open house isn't all that difficult either. It's not that hard to control what's going on. Open houses should have a two-agent team maintaining the open house, so one can control the door and only let one or two families in at a time and the other can get the buyer to sign in for security reasons and confirm follow up. The home tour can be conducted shortly after asking the buyer some pre-qualifying questions.

Now that you have decided to have an open house, pull out all the stops, make it an event and get tons of exposure. Promote the open house to your email list as usually this provides a 200% ROI. Consider having a themed open house. Have the open house catered to make it more interesting. Nobody can resist free food! They will be talking about your event and your home for weeks!

Open house signs should be used strategically to draw traffic to your open house. Use multiple types of signs that are visible and legible from a distance and place directional signs to advertise in a five block radius to reach a wider audience.

Spruce up the front door to make a great first impression. Bring in a housekeeper or professional organizer. Make sure the house is ready for its close up. Declutter. Depersonalize. Keep the scent neutral and stage like a pro!

Valuables should always be put away. Secure prescription medications, money, jewellery and blank checks. Do not just stash them in a drawer. Lock them away.

There are three handouts every agent should market for the seller and provide to the buyer at an open house:

1. *Mortgage loan breakdown:* Helps prospects understand the potential costs of financing the open house property. Also provide a single sheet of key terms and mortgage phrases which can be extremely helpful to both first-time buyers and move-up buyers who haven't purchased a home in a while.

2. *Media promos:* Glossary or colour brochure of the featured home, photo album of the home showing it year-round, list the upgrades and extras. You may also want to have a computer or laptop with the featured home video tour.

3. *Neighbourhood information handout:* Note local schools, grocery stores, community centres or restaurants and the "walk score" of the home. Proximity of transit, major highways, etc.

Don't forget to ask your agent to also hold an 'Agents Open House!' Your agent should build a list of every agent that has sold a house in the neighbourhood in the past year, as well as all the active buyer agents in the area, and call them to personally invite them to the event. Have refreshments and hors d'oeuvres ready for your guests. This leaves a lasting positive impression!

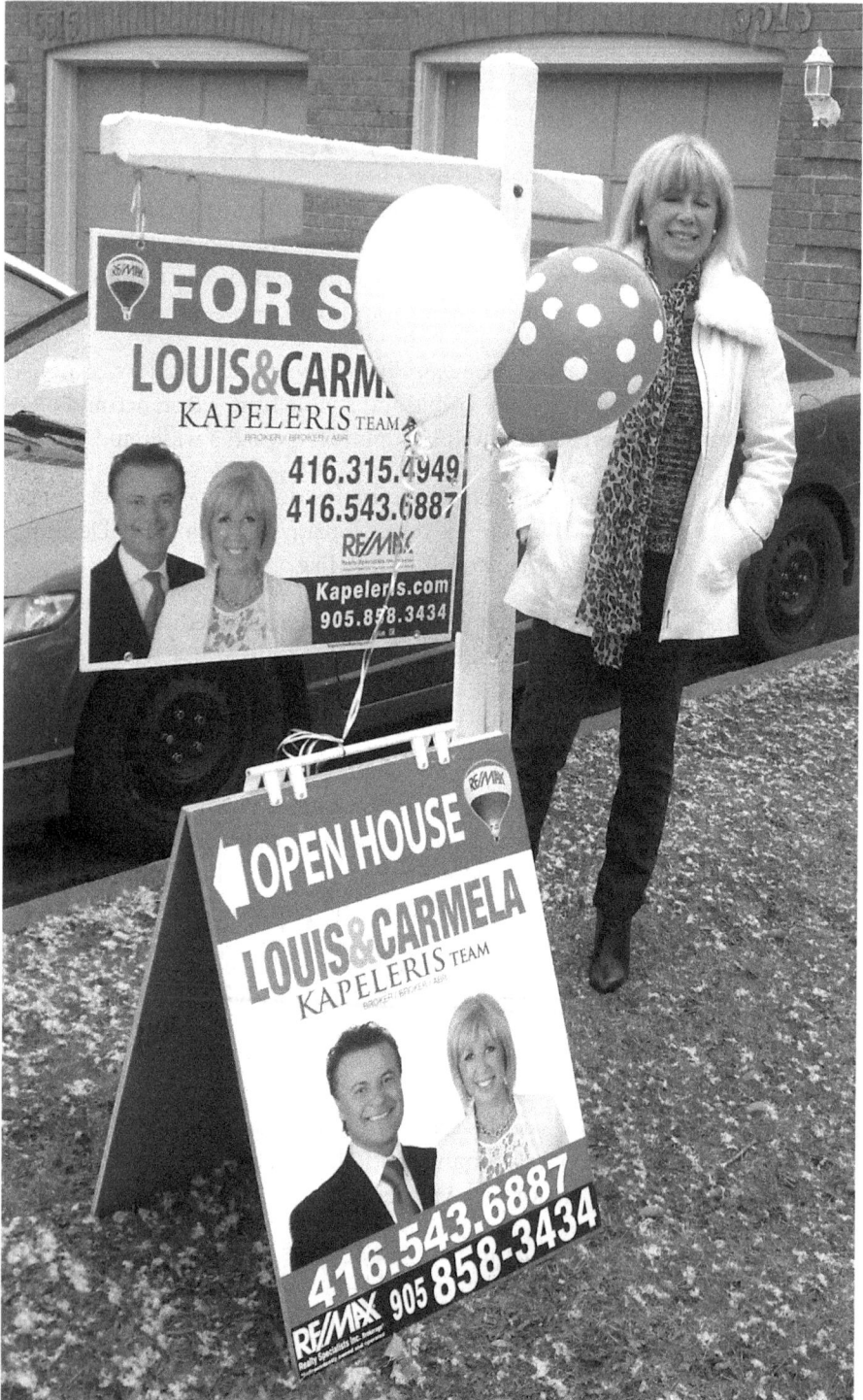

Chapter 14: How to pay off your mortgage faster

If you're thinking of eventually moving from a condo to a house, it only makes sense to work on building the equity on your current home so that you will have more to put towards a down payment on your next home.

Here is some vital info to consider when getting a mortgage:

What is the difference between a mortgage broker and a bank? Banks have one product (mortgage offer), while mortgage brokers have access to 50 or 60 lenders, including the big banks and they can help you compare all these products, understand all the options and penalty calculators. It's not always about the mortgage interest rate. What is more important is the terms and flexibility of the product. People always forget when applying for a mortgage with a bank or lender to always ask these two questions:

- *How do you calculate the penalty payments?*
- *What are my pre-payment privileges?*

Some pre-payments on a mortgage can be 10%,15%, others are 20%. These pre-payment privileges are lump sums of money you can put down against the principal part of your mortgage. Some mortgages allow you to only contribute on the anniversary date of the mortgage. That is, if you have a 5-year mortgage for $100,000, then once a year you can put 10% or $10,000 towards your principal if you have the extra cash savings. Some other mortgages, allow a pre-payment option every payment date. So make sure you ask and find out.

You can end up losing more money on bad terms instead of higher rates. For example: If a mortgage rate is five basis points higher, it could cost you an extra $8 or $9 a month, whereas bad penalty programs at the end can cost you tens of thousands of dollars.

How can a mortgage be paid off faster without paying a prepayment charge? A mortgage is a big commitment. Most mortgages are paid over 25 or 30 years' amortizations, but there are some tips and incentives that can help you pay it off faster. Reducing the number of years that you make mortgage payments can add up to big savings!

Try to increase your payments! Some mortgages let you increase your payment amount by up to 100% of the original regular payment, at any time over the mortgage term. This allows you to pay down your principal faster. For example, if you increased your mortgage payment amount by $170 from $830 to $1,000, you could save almost $48,000 in interest over the entire amortization period of your mortgage. You could also pay off your mortgage about eight years earlier.

Try to increase your payment frequency! You can make your regular mortgage payments more often, which saves you money in interest as your principal is paid down faster. For example, if you made accelerated bi-weekly payments of $415 instead of monthly payments of $830, you could save almost $27,000 in interest over the entire amortization period of your mortgage. This would allow you to pay off your mortgage about 4.5 years sooner.

Try to prepay at renewal! You can pay as much as possible at renewal. Check if your mortgage has become open at the end of the mortgage term. This means you can pay as much as you want on your mortgage before you renew. For example, if you chose a 5-year, fixed-rate term, and made a $10,000 lump-sum payment every time your mortgage came up for renewal, you would save about $37,481 in interest over the entire amortization period of your mortgage, allowing you to pay off your mortgage about six years sooner.

Mortgage tip When you put your home up for sale, make sure you check the status of your mortgage with your bank or lender. Find out if you can 'port the mortgage'—i.e. transfer it to another property. Ask how much you qualify to increase that mortgage and what are the blended payments and terms of the new mortgage. If you are not buying right away or renting, find out when the mortgage expires, how long they will hold the mortgage and rate, and what the penalty fees are for early termination.

Important note: These mortgage calculations are ballpark figures. All estimations are approximate and vary in each province and country. Please contact your local bank or lender for an accurate, personalized calculation and private consultation based on your housing and mortgage needs.

Chapter 15: There's an offer on your home — now what? Holding back offers

Congrats! You have an offer on your house!

There are different strategies that can be used when it comes to receiving an offer on your home. In a regular market, it usually takes upwards of 30 days to get a signed and sealed offer on a residential listing.

The expected protocol is the buyer's agent always calls the listing agent at their office and registers the offer. The buyer and their agent can choose to email or fax their offer or be present at the offer presentation which is usually at the seller's house or the seller's agent's office.

It is always better for the buyer's representative to be present to negotiate the offer for their buyer. Buyers are never present at the presentation. It is only the sellers, the sellers' agents and the buyers agents (if required) who are present to discuss the offer.

There are many strategies used in the negotiations. The offer when presented can be accepted, rejected or counter offered by the seller on the guidance and advice of the seller's agent. In most cases, unless it is a low ball offer, it is counter offered with an irrevocable date, meaning a specific time or date the buyer needs to answer by in writing.

The buyer agent will then contact the buyers and go to their home with the sign back. They can either accept, counter offer or reject. Usually both buyers and sellers negotiate on behalf of their agents till they reach an agreement on price, deposit, closing date, chattels included and all other terms and conditions.

For low ball offers, the seller will sometimes refuse to sign the offer till the buyer and their agent come back with a more reasonable price offer.

Then there is a buyers' market when the houses on the market outnumber the buyers by the dozens. The houses in a buyers' market may stay on the market from six months to a year or longer before receiving an offer and finally selling.

Let's fast pace to today's seller markets. A sellers' market means there are more buyers than there are houses to sell (inventory). In a sellers' market, we can experience multiple offers, more than one bidder on the same house, sometimes up to 20 bidders at once on the same house. In this situation, offers come in usually right away, within 24 to 48 hours.

Holding back offers

Hence the solution, virtually every house listed for sale these days in a sellers' market comes with a designated offer date, or you could say that the listing has a 'hold back date' on offers. What does that mean? Well, a hold back on offers usually happens in a red hot real estate market when the inventory is so low that the offers come in too quickly which doesn't give the seller/agent enough time to market the home and get all potential buyers through. Therefore, there is a hold back date which usually generates multiple offers and maximizes the sale price on a home.

Which is a good thing for everybody except the buyers and the buyer agents, who sometimes end up working with a buyer for months on end making offers before they actually win their dream home.

The next question for both sellers and buyers would be: how long does a hold back on offers usually last? Typically, most offer dates are about 5-7 days after the listing comes out. This is *not* a coincidence. The seller and seller's agent want to allow at least a full weekend to pass after listing, thus exposing the home via the public open house and give all buyers time to see the home, as well as go back for a second viewing if needed with family member or home inspector to do a pre-inspection on the home and make a firm offer with no condition.

It may seem that the buyer is under pressure to act quickly, but in a fast-paced real estate market, the buyer usually gets a new listing emailed to him or her the very day it comes out and then goes to see the property that evening. That buyer might say 'okay, we are interested' that very evening and thus 'quick' could mean only eight hours after the listing hits the market.

Waiting around for a full week can seem like slow torture to both eager buyers as well as anxious sellers who want to get on with the sale. Yet that is just the way real estate deals play out in the industry. The seller's realtor would not be helping their client if they grabbed the first offer that came along without trying to go for the highest bid. They want top dollar on the property just as the seller does.

But what about the alternative? In the above scenario, we talked about offers that are reviewed too quickly. But how about when offers are held back too long? Three undesirable scenarios can occur:

- A seller may risk having the buyer pool cool off as the initial excitement fades.

- It leaves the door open for buyers to have second thoughts and change their minds about buying.

- Another property may come on the market that the buyer likes better.

Holding back on offers is one of the commonly used maneuvers in real estate. None of us really like the system we have in place or the low inventory situation. But just know that if you are a highly frustrated buyer, it helps to get a better perspective of the sale by putting the shoe on the other foot and asking yourself if you wouldn't hold back offers if *you* were a seller in a hot sellers' market.

"The miracle of gratitude is that it shifts your perception to such an extent that it changes the world you see."

– Dr. Robert Holden

Chapter 16: Selling your home—for seniors

When seniors make the decision to sell their homes, it is often because of the need to downsize for convenience, health and safety reasons. Communal living in senior residences eases social isolation that many seniors experience after retirement. Whether the move is for pleasant reasons or not, the process of selling the house and all the 'stuff' inside it can be daunting. As an Accredited Seniors Agent, I have met many seniors making the transition to new homes, and all too often I see fear and frustration.

A senior—or a person who cares for one—can begin the process of moving to a new home/lifestyle by gathering information through the many professionals who are specifically trained in providing seniors' services. They can help prepare a home for sale, sell and pack personal property, and assist with arranging finances related to the move.

A Senior Financial Planner can assess and advise a senior client on their current assets and future housing options.

A realtor will help design a game plan for the sale of the house and recommend trusted professionals for any needed repairs and updates to make it 'show' to advantage and increase its worth to buyers. It is critical to find a real estate agent who is knowledgeable about the specialized needs of seniors. Accredited Seniors Agents are trained and experienced in senior housing options. They can steer you away from schemes and scams and explain the implications of various real estate-related financial transactions.

Seven mistakes retired people make

1. *Not planning ahead:* Many seniors aren't aware of or fail to accurately calculate how much money they will need when they retire. Most people plan finances for 10 or 20 years after retirement, but they should really plan as if they will live to 100. Why 100? Well, apart from the general cost of day-to-day living, seniors also have to consider the cost of medical expenses, retirement home living, assisted living, or in-home care. Hence, when calculating retirement income, it is important to plan for a longer period and additional contingencies.

2. *Going it alone:* Seniors may not seek professional help to figure out their retirement plans or to sell their home. Sometimes they avoid thinking about retirement altogether and are reluctant to move from their homes even when it has become increasingly difficult to stay in their current residence.

It's a good idea to look for a financial planner, realtor, accountant, and other professionals who specialize in seniors' needs and put retirement plans in place well in advance. Even if their help is not needed immediately, it will be in the future. It is comforting to know that a plan is in place should circumstances change.

3. *Too many cooks:* If there are a number of friends and family guiding you with your retirement plans, it can lead to confusion with several differing opinions. It is a good idea to have your family present at consultations, but ultimately the final decision is yours.

4. *Selling before confirming a future residence:* Moving is stressful enough, but you don't want to be uprooted twice before you settle into the new home. A real estate agent who specializes in seniors will be able to weigh your options and estimate your net from the real estate closing so you can make your post-sale arrangements. With their expertise, they will be able to secure and co-ordinate both your closing dates to make your transition as smooth as possible.

5. *Keeping the clutter:* Too much clutter can kill a sale. You don't want to convey the lived-in look, but rather have the bare minimum in terms of furnishings, with no accessories and knickknacks to distract from the 'bones' of the home. This is an ideal time to go through your treasures of a lifetime and start sharing them with the family and close friends who will appreciate them. What you intend to take to your new home could be packed up and kept in temporary storage or with family or friends. It will give you a jump start on your packing.

6. *Not opting for a senior-oriented real estate agent:* Seniors face a different set of issues when selling their homes compared to younger people. For example, there are options available that could allow seniors to stay in their home and remodel or make modifications designed for comfort and ease of living. In real estate, mistakes can be very costly and for that reason seniors should consult with real estate specialists who can discuss their particular needs and make recommendations.

7. *Don't put all your eggs in one basket:* Focusing solely on the sale of your house as a retirement income option can be dangerous. Instead, with advice from a retirement financial specialist, retirees should have a mix of cash and low-risk investments, as well as longer-term investments such as real estate.

Companies that Help Seniors

A Specialized Seniors Agent plays an important role in helping their client hire a professional Senior Move Manager. These companies assist older adults and their families with what is often as much of an emotional decision as it is a physical relocation. These specialized agents have a background in gerontology, social work, psychology and health care.

- The services that these senior moving professionals can help with are:

- Developing an "age in place" plan or an overall moving plan

- Organizing, sorting, downsizing

- Arranging profitable disposal of unwanted items by consignment, estate sale, auction, donation or combination

- Related services such as cleaning, waste removal, shopping

- Arranging shipments and storage

- Interview, schedule and oversee movers

- Supervise and oversee professional packing

- Unpacking and setting up the new home

In other cases, a Specialized Seniors Agent will sometimes find situations where the client is no longer living in the home and hence the agent becomes the go-to expert, the conductor of everything in the transaction. There are many cases where the seniors agent helps the senior client with finding their next home, whether it's a private household, a retirement residence or any of the other discussed options the client has open to them. The job of a seniors agent encompasses many things and the realtor may be wearing many hats in this case. The hope is to build up a mutual relationship of trust, respect and lasting friendships.

Chapter 17: Downsizing/selling: when should I be thinking of this?

Downsizing your lifestyle as a whole, even when you have a family or if you're a young couple, can be a great way to save money, cut expenses and live simpler. But you don't have to be ready to retire or be a senior to downsize. More and more people are turning to renting or smaller homes to save money and as a way of pulling out their equity and using their cash to be more financially independent and efficient.

Here are some more reasons why it may make sense to downsize:

- *Change in income/tight financial situation:* You are paying too much or suffer a loss of income and feel the squeeze and need to cut costs. Your priorities have changed.

- *Travel:* You have a job that allows you to travel frequently for long periods of time and you don't want to have to maintain a big place.

- *Tired of the tedious commute* and spending way too much time on the road and money on gas. Makes sense to move to a smaller place closer to work and save money at the same time.

- *Illness or health concerns:* Your physical health may have changed due to surgery, injury or other reasons and the stairs, the cleaning and upkeep of a larger house may be hard for you. You realize that you need to alter your living conditions till you get better and so downsizing makes sense.

In many cases, downsizing helps you build a retirement fund or nest egg for the future. Whether you are a senior, empty nester or have opted for early retirement or just want to travel and don't want the responsibilities or upkeep that a bigger property entails, rarely is selling one's home an easy decision.

Documents needed for downsizing

Let's now take a look at the documents a realtor requires from the seller when they want to sell their home/downsize.

- Deed to the home
- Survey of the house
- Mortgage documents if any
- House inspection if one has been recently done
- Power of Attorney if one exists

- Current tax bill
- Utility bills
- Copy of permit for any additions that were done (new roof, water softener, etc.)
- Copy of any renovations that were done
- Keys for lockbox
- Features/history of the home
- Seasonal/garden pictures
- Downsizing property search information
- Info regarding alternate living arrangements

Checklist for selling/downsizing for seniors

Realtors who specialize in working with older couples who are thinking of downsizing/selling know that a listing appointment is in most cases a three-step process.

- *1st step:* Is more of a social visit to get to know the older couple and their family and understand their concerns. The aim is to build a trustworthy relationship.

- *2nd step:* Is to talk about housing options, ideas, strategy and the sale of their home.

- *3rd step:* Return visit to prepare the property and sale documents and have the house officially listed. Start marketing the home. Assist and schedule appointment to view downsizing properties or seniors new housing arrangements.

The senior client or downsizer is probably seeking the advice or opinions of their adult children or trusted friends, hence it is very important that these individuals be present at all appointments, if possible. It helps to have all decision makers in the process to be on the same page, and be present when key decisions are made, to avoid misunderstandings and slowing of the process. Adult children generally become involved in their parent/s home sale in some way or the other about 80% of the time.

Then there is the special case of a senior who is living independently and must consider the reality of moving out of their house into an alternate residence. I have prepared a self-help chart that together with their adult child or other concerned individual could consider referring to when making this crucial decision.

Self-Help Chart

	Yes / No	Sometimes
Do I need live-in help?		
Do I have help with housekeeping, cooking, shopping?		
Can I still work in my garden, cut grass, shovel snow?		
Am I able to go up and down the stairs?		
Is the house just too big for me?		
Does the house require expensive repairs?		
Do I need assistance with personal grooming? Paper work?		
Can I afford living here? Utilities, bills, etc.		
Do I feel safe in my home? Alarm, med alert		
Do I feel isolated, lonely?		
Do I want to leave my neighbourhood?		
Reasons to Stay	**Reasons to Move**	

If the senior decides to live independently in their own home or downsize or move to a residence/nursing care, then the above chart will help in pinpointing their needs and what works for them.

Downsizing tips: For more info on downsizing/selling—please refer to *Chapter 2: Make a 'prep' plan and To-Do list.*

Chapter 18: Real estate income—building a nest egg!

Real Estate can be a highly desirable retirement vehicle. It is one of the easiest ways to generate income as you prepare to retire. It all boils down to two simple questions: How soon can you retire? and how much money do you need to live on?

First thing is—Do the math on your mortgage. You could consider a cash-in refinancing to a shorter-term loan. Say you have $200,000 on your mortgage and 20 years left on a 30-year mortgage at an interest rate of 5%. Refinancing your mortgage to 15 years at 3% by putting in $50,000 to shave off five years would cut the monthly payment from $1,381 to $1,074. At the same time, keep up the original payment, and the loan will be paid off in 11 years, plus you'll save $10,300 in interest.

Another retirement option is to "cash in" on your home. Real estate in Canada has enjoyed an enormous boom in recent years, and that has allowed many long-time homeowners to build significant wealth through property appreciation and home equity.

If your home is upscale and expensive to maintain, you could add to your cash savings by downsizing or relocating to a relatively 'cheaper' area. Some homeowners sell modest-sized homes and buy two-bedroom condos nearby, realizing a net profit of $200,000 to $300,000 in today's booming real estate market.

A retired couple in their 60s took advantage of Toronto's hot housing market to top up their nest egg. They sold their semi-detached home for $770,000 and bought a remodeled home in a desirable neighbourhood near the lake for $610,000. They netted more than $100,000 after costs. They could have bought a less expensive home but instead they chose to bank $100,000 and allow higher growth equity on their new home.

The equity in your home can also provide a back-up plan for income on savings should you ever need it. If you stay put in your home, you can cover necessary expenses by borrowing against it with a reverse mortgage or home equity line of credit—but this should only be considered as a last resort, because it puts a lien on your home. Later in life, should you move into a retirement or nursing home, the costs of living in these facilities can be covered for years from the sale proceeds of your house.

Rental properties can add an extra stream of income to your retirement portfolio. Buying a property or two could provide enough income to allow you to retire sooner. An investor can retire and live off the income generated from his/her rental properties. However, you'll need to ensure your rentals become a steady, positive cash flow throughout your retired life. You don't want a rental property to become a drain on your retirement funds.

Always keep in mind that your main goal is getting rid of debt, and not just making it more manageable. As you approach retirement it's critical to only borrow for productive purposes like buying a home or other appreciating assets. Low rates can make the difference and make buying investments more affordable, but they won't turn bad debt into good debt.

Remember to seek sound financial advice from a registered, qualified financial consultant or accountant before making any decisions on real estate investment and retirement funding.

"Real estate cannot be lost or stolen,
nor can it be carried away.
Purchased with common sense,
paid for in full and managed with reasonable care,
it is about the safest investment in the world."

– Franklin D. Roosevelt

SECTION II THE BUYER

Chapter 19: Buying versus renting

If you're struggling with whether to buy versus rent, home ownership is always the key deciding factor. By renting, you are paying your landlord's mortgage! Put your hard earned money towards building home equity and grow your life savings.

Owning a home forces you to save, since as a homeowner, you have to pay your mortgage every month. Hence you are routinely putting money away instead of squandering it on impulse buys that do not really appreciate in value. Rent is money that just flies out the window. Whereas your monthly mortgage payments on the other hand are going towards building equity on your property that you can tap into for kids' college expenses, retirement, renovation and/or income producing properties.

Eventually, as a property owner, you can sell your home or condo, even if the mortgage is not paid off, for considerably more than you purchased it, as the home will appreciate in time. You will make a profit from the sale, even after subtracting the costs of your monthly mortgage interest payments.

When you **own** a home there is potential to earn rental income. The easiest way to do this is by renting out part or all of the property. You might rent out the basement or a bedroom to a friend or relative. You can look into the 'sharing economy' and take in short-term renters via Airbnb, VRBO, or another house-sharing platform. All this can partially or totally offset your mortgage, property tax, and insurance payments.

Another great reason to own your residential property is to avoid the fate of renters who may face an unexpected eviction notice if their landlord suddenly decides to sell the house or condo, rent it to someone else, or end the lease. Also rental payments can go up where mortgage payments stay fixed. For these reasons, home ownership offers both security and stability.

Mortgage rates have never been this low (at time of going to press). Lock in a low monthly payment, and you've just taken a huge step in protecting yourself against inflation. You can save money and get tax breaks too, just for making your home more energy efficient. Buying those new windows for your home may be written off at the end of the year along with other energy efficient remedies.

When you buy a home—it'll be yours! You own it! Some rentals come with a big list of do's and don'ts. For instance, if you're expecting an addition to the family and you own your home, you could easily convert or build a nursery, move walls, build an extension if zoning permits and can have the type of kitchen and bathrooms you want. You don't have to ask permission to paint or put a nail in the wall. For renters, these types of changes are often impossible. You'll feel more relaxed in your own place if you own it than if you rent.

Most rentals don't allow pets, smoking, etc. Some allow small animals, but if you have a large family dog, it's likely to be a problem finding a rental space.

Before you begin to spend your Sundays at open houses, there are a few things you might want to consider first, regarding the type of home are looking for. Look at the following checklist.

New Home Checklist		
How important is home ownership for you?		
Where do you want to live?		
Do you see yourself in a big city, suburb, or rural area?		
What kind of housing are you looking for?		
How much can you afford?		
How soon do you think you'll move again?		
Do you plan on relocating in the next few years, or are you staying put?		
Are you willing to move to a different city if you're priced out of where you live now?		
What kinds of amenities would you like?		
Would you renovate a fixer upper?		
Would you rent out part of your home?		
Are you qualified for a mortgage by the bank?		
Who will be on the title / mortgage?		

In a nutshell, this is the ideal checklist for a buyer considering residential accommodation:

- Write down the pros and cons of a renting vs. buying scenario.

- Look at your finances, savings and down-payment.

- Go to the bank and see what type of mortgage you qualify for.

- Choose a realtor who explains the annual costs of buying

Very soon you will be on your way to building your life savings and equity through home ownership.

"Real Estate is the best investment in the world because it is the only thing they're not making anymore."

– Will Rogers

Chapter 20: Buying a Condo—should I, should I not?

As the prices of single family houses rise, many home buyers look at purchasing a condominium as an alternative. First time buyers like the lower prices, which makes entry into the real estate market easier for them.

Seniors consider the low maintenance aspect of a smaller home and the ability to be in a community catering to their lifestyle. For them, condos ease social isolation, yet they have the privacy of their own home.

One of the strong advantages of condo-living is the relative security that the building provides, especially for those who travel frequently.

When you purchase a condominium, you purchase the title to your own individual unit in a multi-unit property. You share in the ownership of the land and other common property with all the other unit owners.

Owing a condo does offer you pride of ownership, freedom to make interior changes and enhancements to your unit, which is a way of investing in your own home and building equity!

Some pre-construction condo projects are more successful than others in terms of capital appreciation and length of time it takes to sell the condo after it hits the real estate market. (See *Chapter 35: Are buyer assignments legal?*)

Here are some advantages to condo ownership:

• Monthly cost of owning is often less than renting and you own the property.

• Peace of mind without the worry of a driveway to clear in the winter or grass to cut in the summer. Upkeep of the yard and common facilities is included in the maintenance fee.

• Some condos offer amenities such as a swimming pool, tennis courts, saunas, whirlpools, exercise facilities, health spas and party rooms (these services may not be otherwise affordable)

Condos are not for everyone. Due to a larger concentration of people, you may experience problems with the "5 p's": pets, parties, parking, personality and people. If any one of these considerations is likely to become your pet peeve, then perhaps you need to rethink the idea of purchasing a condo before committing. Here are some disadvantages that condo dwellers experience:

- Condo maintenance fees increase regularly.

- You may not be able to decide when maintenance and repairs need to be done. Or have a say in the décor and colour schemes in common areas.

- Less privacy than in a detached home, as you would be living in relatively close proximity to others.

- Noise levels: pets and kids may be heard through walls and ceilings. If you are easily disturbed by these sounds, you might like to consider a building listed as 'adult-lifestyle only.'

- Parking: There may not be enough parking spaces for guests and visitors. Or even for a second/additional vehicle.

"Buy on the fringe and wait.
Buy land near a growing city!
Buy real estate when other people want to sell.
Hold what you buy!"

– John Jacob Astor - 1763

Chapter 21: The adventures of the Millennial buyer

Today's Millennials or Gen Y kids (born between 1980-2000) are having trouble earning creditable pay cheques to put toward a mortgage. Their eligibility for mortgages is further impacted by the fact that banks have tightened up lending rules. Add to this a steady 10-year rise in house prices across Canada and it is no surprise Gen Y is finding it hard to buy their first home.

Five main obstacles facing Millennials and Gen Y's considering buying a home today are:

• Not qualifying for a mortgage

• Lacking funds for a down payment

• Not finding a home that meets their needs and budget

• Not earning enough to afford the monthly mortgage payments

Another big obstacle is a little something called 'student debt.' Young adults are saddled with student loan repayments for many years after leaving college and university. Credit card debt is another negative factor in credit worthiness and this is in large part due to spending habits.

Here are some helpful suggestions for Gen Y homebuyers:

• Start saving for a home down payment early.

• Create a "down payment fund" by setting up automatic transfers each month into a high interest savings account.

• Take advantage of the federal government's Home Buyers' Plan, which lets you borrow up to $25,000 from your RRSP.

• Dump those high-interest credit cards! Borrowing to buy a place to live in is seen by banks as a much safer investment than credit cards. And the interest rates are considerably lower.

• Stop renting. Rent payments go straight into the pocket of the landlord. At the end of the lease period, you have got nothing to show for it. Some Gen Y's are willing to move in with their parents temporarily or take a second job in order to achieve their dream of home ownership.

The key is to start small. Over 75% of Gen Y's are buying 500-600 sq ft condos, centrally located with stainless steel appliances and public amenities. Preferred locations are close to work and transit hubs. This eliminates the need for a car and extra expenses.

A good strategy for new buyers is to purchase new or pre-construction condos. You then make small deposits towards your down payment over a period of 2-5 years. When the condo is built and ready to be occupied, your condo investment has increased in value by at least 10% - 20% by the time you are ready to move in. If you are willing to wait it out, I'd say that is a great first time home investment.

"If you want to succeed
you should strike out on new paths,
rather than travel the worn paths
of accepted success."

– John D. Rockefeller

Chapter 22: Saving money to buy a home

Saving money to buy a home is all about priorities. It is all up to you! Are you willing to tighten your belt and save for a house?

First try to identify areas where you can cut back and then put the money saved into a tax-free savings account. Do some research about the type of home you are considering and how much it will cost. Create a budget so you have a rough idea of how much you need for the cost of living and how much you can put aside to save for a home.

Here are some great quick tips that may save you thousands of dollars to start.

- *Pay off your credit card debt:* If you are carrying a credit card balance of $5,000 at 19% interest, you are paying almost $1,000 a year to your credit card company in interest. Pay it off and don't use the card again! If you do, pay the balance off monthly as soon as you get your statement.

- *Try not to use Interac/debit card:* By using cash instead of your debit card you can keep track of your expenses.

- *Take a lunch to work instead of eating out:* If you buy lunch for $7 every working day of the year, you will end up spending over $1,800 a year. Try not to eat out.

- *Purchasing a vehicle:* Buy a quality used vehicle that is still under warranty rather than a new one. A new $28,000 car will lose about $17,000 dollars of value in the first four years you own it. Buying a used car saves you tens of thousands of dollars. If you have two cars, consider getting rid of one car. You could look at moving closer to where you or your partner works. You could consider walking, carpooling or taking transit (80% cheaper than owning a car).

- *Look for cheaper ways to do things:* This is how smart people save a lot of money. Here are some great examples:

- *Stick to your grocery list:* Don't always buy brand names. Shopping at discount grocery stores can save you 10% on your groceries and buying your produce at a produce store can save you 32%.

- *Save your change:* At the end of each day, put your loose change into a jar.

- *Give yourself an allowance* and stick with it.

- *Don't carry a lot of cash or credit cards in your wallet:* Impulse spending is harder if you have to go to the bank machine to get money.

- *Family entertainment:* If you have a busy family, you can really save money if you eat at home more often (and this includes buying less snacks and drinks on the run), and look for fun things to do around your community that are free or don't cost very much.

- *Do you go out to a lot of movies?* Try renting or sticking with cable. Some people are now even dropping their cable in favor of watching shows online.

- *Do you buy a lot of new books?* Try the library.

- *Make your own coffee:* Instead of buying a coffee every day, make your own. If you spend only $2 on a cup of coffee every working day, that adds up to $500 per year.

- *Do you take expensive vacations?* Try something less expensive or closer to home for a while.

If you are able to work some of these changes into your lifestyle, you will definitely save money. A Savings account can be a great place to save your down payment money. Check with your bank for savings options that suit your needs.

Chapter 23: How much house can I afford?

Are you struggling with the question of how much house you can afford? This would depend on your 'gross debt service ratio.' Here is a quick way to figure that out:

Add up your before-tax monthly income and multiply it by 32% and the total equals the monthly housing payments you can AFFORD.

Here is the equation:

GROSS MONTHLY INCOME x 32%
= TOTAL MONTHLY HOUSING PAYMENTS

This 'total' figure includes the mortgage and other costs such as:

• Monthly property taxes
• Heating
• Insurance
• Condo Fees

Keep in mind that this 'total' amount should not be more than 32% of your gross monthly income.

Then there are onetime costs associated with the purchase of a house, which must be taken into consideration. These are:

• Home inspection
• Lawyers' fees
• Moving costs
• HST on new housing

To figure out your maximum home price, you must figure out:

• The size of your down payment
• Interest rates
• Number of years on your mortgage

Crunch the numbers yourself or with the assistance of your realtor or financial consultant before you go to see a mortgage specialist, and definitely before you go house hunting! Knowing how much house you can afford narrows your focus to what is feasible and helps you enjoy the experience of looking for a new home.

How much down payment do I need?

The amount of mortgage that you can qualify for with the bank or lender is usually based on a couple's combined income, debt (debt ratio) and amount of down payment—i.e. 5%, 10%, 15% down payment are subject to CMHC insurance fees. A 20% down payment is considered a conventional mortgage and it is not subject to CMHC fees.

Before February 15th, 2016, if you bought a house with the purchase price of $700,000, you could put down a minimum down payment of 5% providing you could qualify for the mortgage with your income. So 5% x $700,000 = $35,000 minimum 5% down payment.

After February 15th, 2016, if you bought a house with the purchase price of $700,000, you could only put 5% down payment on the first $500,000 which is = $25,000.

The remainder of the purchase price of $200,000 had to be 10% down payment, which = $20,0000 for a total down payment of $45,000.

The combined percentage equals 6.4% of $700,000 = $45,000. For anyone buying a home for $700,000, the down payment increased by $10,000, from $35,0000 to $45,000 according to the new mortgage rules.

The first $500,000 is 5%. Anything above that is 10%. For a million dollars and up, down payment is 20%. (*See the following illustration*)

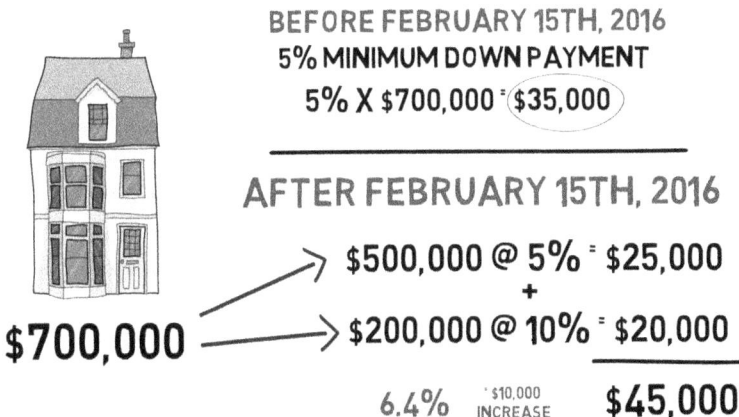

BEFORE FEBRUARY 15TH, 2016
5% MINIMUM DOWN PAYMENT
5% X $700,000 = $35,000

AFTER FEBRUARY 15TH, 2016

$700,000

> $500,000 @ 5% = $25,000
+
> $200,000 @ 10% = $20,000

6.4% * $10,000 INCREASE **$45,000**

Chapter 24: Shopping for a mortgage

There are many types and options for mortgages available. Your best bet is to contact a mortgage broker and shop around for the type of mortgage that suits you.

Here are some points to keep in mind when considering mortgage options:

- *The power of pre-payment privileges.* There are a number of factors to consider when deciding whether to pre-pay your mortgage. Make sure you qualify for this option.

- *Flexibility versus rate.* Buyers are usually hung up on the interest rate of the mortgage offer. But there are several other important factors to consider. First of all is the mortgage flexible. In what ways? Find out and use your mortgage broker's experience and advice to figure the best option for you.

- *Bank or broker?* Banks offer a single mortgage package to all their clients. Whereas a mortgage broker will shop around to find you the best deal. Brokers are not tied to any particular financial institution and are hence free to shop around, compare and pick the ideal deal for their client.

- *Mortgage insurance premium added to monthly payments.* In most cases mortgage insurance premiums can be added to your mortgage and included in your monthly payments. Usually the higher the down payment, the lower the premium. How are mortgage insurance premiums calculated? Some mortgage brokers offer a mortgage premium calculator on their websites that people can go to and do their own calculations. Try yourmortgageyourway. com

- *Mortgage loans for the self-employed.* Genworth Canada offers a program designed for self-employed borrowers who are unable to provide traditional income verification but have a proven two-year history of managing their credit and finances responsibly. Eligible borrowers typically own a small size business for a minimum of two years, which can be confirmed via a third-party arm's length document. In addition, the borrower is required to declare their annual income and annual business revenue, which should be reasonable based on the industry, length of operation and type of business. Check with your bank or lender for other mortgage programs for self-employed business people.

- *Mortgage program for secondary homes?* Genworth Canada offers mortgage loans for second homes with less than 20% down, whether it's a second home in the city to reduce that weekly commute or a cottage at the lake for weekend getaways. With the vacation/secondary homes program, Canadians can now purchase a second home with an affordable monthly payment with only 5% down payment.

- *Home improvement value program:* Canadian Mortgage and Housing Corporation has a program called Purchase Plus Improvements, which allows a consumer to obtain estimates for work that needs to be done to the home. They will take the home improvement expenses and add the amount "as improved value" onto the mortgage.

  CMHC also provides tools online for the consumers to access their credit report. Further they will explain and help you understand and improve your rating.

- *Green home program.* CMHC provides homeowners with a 10% premium rebate on mortgage insurance if they show proof of energy-efficient, 'green' measures undertaken to update their home.

- *Ontario Renovates.* This CMHC program provides financial assistance to low income homeowners by way of a forgivable loan, used in order to repair their home while improving the energy-efficiency of the unit, create secondary suites to increase accessibility, remediate overcrowding, help victims of violence. This program serves: homeowners; renters; seniors; persons with disabilities; victims of family violence.

  Forgivable loan, also called a soft second is a form of loan in which its entirety or a portion of it, can be forgiven or deferred for a period of time by the lender when certain conditions are met.

  Types of home repairs that may be eligible for the Ontario Renovates Program include:

  Heating systems, chimneys, doors and windows, foundations, roofs, walls, floors and ceilings, plumbing, septic system, vents, louvres, well wall and well drilling, electrical systems (excluding installation of solar panels)

  Types of accessibility repairs that may be eligible for Ontarian Renovates Program include: ramps, handrails, chair and bath lifts, height adjustment to countertops, doorbells/fire alarms.

- *Homeownership Assistance programs.* A program currently in effect in the Region of Peel is the Peel Affordable Home Ownership Program, which is designed to provide low to moderate income residents currently renting a unit in the Region of Peel (Brampton, Caledon or Mississauga) with an opportunity to qualify for down payment loan assistance to buy a home in Peel Region. This program may assist eligible applications who have a maximum gross (pre-tax) household income of $88,900 to purchase a resale home in the Region of Peel up to a maximum purchase price of $330,000. To get more information go to: https://www.peelregion.ca/housing/home-in-peel/

This list is my no means conclusive. New programs may become available in future. It is advisable to do current research on the websites mentioned above or speak to a mortgage broker to find out options available and the best option for you. Good luck!

Note: Information provided on Genworth and CMHC is referenced verbatim and is available on their respective websites.

Chapter 25: Hidden costs of purchasing a home

Homebuyers know that they need money for a deposit, a down payment as well as regular monthly mortgage payments... However, many homebuyers are not aware of the additional hidden costs that they should be prepared to pay when buying a new home: make a note of the figures in your case.

Property valuation fee: Approx. $150 - $200
In order to qualify for a mortgage, lending institutions require the property to be appraised. The buyer or lender hires the property appraiser.

Home inspection fees - Approx. $500
It is usually the buyer's obligation to hire a home inspector to evaluate the condition of the home and obtain a written report. While not mandatory, many people make a home inspection a condition in their offer.

Land transfer tax: Varies based on province/country
A land transfer tax is based on the purchase price. It is up to the buyer to pay the tax. In some cases, first time homebuyers may be exempt from a portion of this cost. You can obtain further details about land transfer tax on provincial or municipal websites to help you estimate the cost. Unlike property taxes, land transfer tax is a onetime cost paid by the purchaser on closing. It is similar to the tax you pay on a store bought item, but due to the size of a home purchase, it can be a significant expense. Use the chart (below) to determine the estimated tax based on your particular purchase price. First time borrowers today, are eligible for a Provincial Maximum Land transfer tax rebate of $2,000 and a Municipal Maximum land transfer rebate of $3,725 for land that contains at least one and not more than two single family residences. For more information and complete details, check with your lawyer to see if this applies to you.

Purchase price of home	Land title transfer fee	First-time homebuyer rebate
Up to and including $55,000	0.5%	Full tax rebate
$55,000 up to and including $227,000	1.0%	Full tax rebate
$227,000 up to and including $250,000	1.0%	$2,000 tax rebate
$250,000 up to and including $400,000	1.5%	$2,000 tax rebate
Over $400,000	2.0%	$2,000 tax rebate

Legal fees and related expenses: Approx. $800 - $2,000
These fees vary by province and country and some are subject to GST or HST. Ensure your lawyer's quote includes all related expenses and disbursements, not just legal fees.

Prepaid property tax and utilities: Approx. $400 - $500
You will be required to reimburse the seller for any prepaid property taxes or utility bills.

Home insurance: Approx. $450/year
Protection for your home and contents.

Title insurance: Approx. $250
Title insurance is optional. Lending institutions normally require the buyer to purchase title insurance to cover any title-related issues that may arise with respect to the property.

Insurance costs for high-ratio mortgages: Variable
If your down payment is less than 20% of the purchase price, you must pay a one-time insurance premium on your mortgage amount. You can pay the premium before closing or it can be added to your mortgage. If it is added to your mortgage, you will have to pay interest.

Chapter 26: Buyer Etiquette – mind your Ps and Qs

There is a proper etiquette involved in the process of purchasing a home. Real estate is a business and there are expectations and 'right ways' of dealing with the parties involved. Buyers, particularly first time ones, may not be aware of some of the do's and don'ts. I have compiled a list of real estate etiquette that lays out the process in a plan.

- *Have a buyer agent.* Once you hire a realtor to assist you with the buying process, that buyer agent should be your go-to agent for this transaction. It is their job to find you a home and to negotiate your sale. Be open and honest with your realtor. If you are not fully open and honest with them, there is no way they can do the best possible job for you! If you don't like a house give your agent your reasons for not liking it. If you are unsure about something, tell them. They may have a solution or have seen the situation before and can help.

- *Mortgage approval.* Tell your buyer agent exactly how much money you want to spend on a home and what mortgage amount has been pre-approved by the bank. This will help narrow down the search to exactly the properties you are looking for.

- *Be on time for a showing.* If for some reason you are going to be late or need to reschedule an appointment, call or text your realtor as soon as possible to let them know. Preparing to show a home requires a lot of coordination and timing. Sellers may need to make child-care arrangements or make sure their dog is out of the house. Sellers will typically leave the home for the time period the showing is scheduled for. Also your realtor may have a number of showings for you, that are on a specific time schedule, so be respectful of everyone's time.

- *How many homes should you see?* Good question! On a single day try to limit the showings to 5 or 6 tops. Any more than that and it starts to get really confusing. Make sure to make notes, name the houses and rate them so it will be easier to remember once you go back to evaluate.

- *Going to open houses.* If you want to go out on a Sunday morning and look at open houses, contact your agent first. When at the open house let the realtor working the open house know you have an agent and give them your agent's business card.

- *Let your agent do the research for you.* Do not visit any new home builders without your realtor. If you do, you could lose the opportunity to have your agent represent you. While driving around if you see a home that catches your eye, write down the address and call your realtor. They will schedule a showing for you promptly.

- *Work with the team.* If your realtor is going on vacation do not call the listing agent to see a listing. Before your realtor goes on vacation they should make plans for their absence. Typically, they will have someone on their team they trust looking after you and their business.

- *Do not approach seller directly.* Last but not least, do not ever attempt to contact the seller directly. You should always go through your realtor. You will look pushy, and it may upset the seller. Remember your realtor should always be there to help, assist and represent you at all times.

"Buy low and sell high.
It's pretty simple.
The problem is knowing
what's low and what's high."

— Jim Rogers

Chapter 27: Buyer beware checklist

Buying a home is a big financial commitment, so it's crucial to know what you're getting into before you put down any money. Here are some facts and tips for buyers to be aware of when they begin the house hunting experience.

When you begin thinking about buying a house, start by calculating how much 'house' you can afford on no more than 32% of your annual salary. This is a clear guideline to make sure you will not over extend yourself on your mortgage and end up being house poor.

Getting a pre-approval on your mortgage will give you more bargaining power when it comes to putting an offer to purchase on your dream home. You will have a clearer picture of what you can afford.

As well as a down payment, be sure you are able to set aside a couple of months' mortgage payment in case of a job loss or other financial emergencies.

Check out your chosen neighbourhood. Drive around and evaluate the traffic and/or transit times from the home to your workplace and to shops (supermarkets, convenience stores, etc.).

Buy a house that is located in a good school district. This will increase the resale value of the house as most buyers have school age children.

Find out the noise level in the neighbourhood during the day versus night. During the weekday versus on the weekend. Are there hospitals, airport, train stations nearby that could impact the noise level even more?

Are there sidewalks, parks and other amenities in the neighbourhood?

What is the neighbourhood culture? Who are your neighbours?

What would your commute be like in the morning, in the afternoon, five days a week for the next several years. How much will it cost you for gas, tolls, etc.

Hire your own home inspector to detect any potential problems in the home. Interview at least two or three inspectors to find the right one. Keep in mind, the home inspection report could also be used as a negotiating tool. That is if essential work needs to be done, the estimated cost of this work can be taken off the asking price for the house or the owner could have the work done.

Do you see any signs of pests? Are there any weird smells or odours? Your home inspector will check the attic and surrounding ground and may see signs of pest activity.

How old is the roof? What condition is it in? When does it need to be replaced? Your home inspector will be able to guide you in this matter.

Check the condition of the front yard. Does the driveway, steps need repair? Are you able to climb those stairs for the next ten or so years that you plan on living in this house?

How old are the appliances? When will they need to be replaced? Do they still have an appliance warranty?

Are there window and window coverings in the house that you can live with? This can cost you tens of thousands of dollars to replace.

Check smoke detectors in the ceilings on each level. Are they the battery type?

Have you factored in the closing costs? What are the property taxes for the house? What is the land transfer tax amount? Make sure you include all the calculations for these factors, so you don't run into any problems on closing.

If you are viewing a condominium, find out the do's and don'ts of the condo complex, what are their and your responsibilities for your unit. Make sure you factor in maintenance fees in your financial calculations and give due consideration to inflation.

Keep in mind if the house is a fixer-upper, the price should be reflective of the work needing to be done and the costs thereof. Even if the location is excellent and all other features of the home are ideal—your dream home could end up being a money pit if there are structural issues or major work has to be done. You and your agent need to negotiate those repairs into the offer and the contract.

Lastly, there is a little thing buyers should beware of called 'buyer's remorse.' Why would a buyer feel remorse when buying something they spent so much time researching and debating? While the answer is different for everyone, when you decide to buy a new home, you're forced to step outside your current comfort zone and confront the unknown. It may stem from fear of making the wrong choice, fear of making a long-term commitment, guilt over extravagance, you may even try to talk yourself out of buying your dream home. Don't! I'm here to tell you this feeling is temporary. It will pass. It is only jitters. If you've gone through all the steps in this book, done your research, are working with the right realtor/team, have set a budget and saved up the money needed—feel good about the purchase you're making, have no regrets and don't second guess yourself. You made the right decision and you're on the right track. You always win with real estate!

Chapter 28: Watch out for real estate and mortgage fraud

Real estate and mortgage fraud comes in various forms but it all boils down to one thing: tricking a financial institution into lending you money when it otherwise would not because you do not qualify. Sometimes the scam is purely about making a profit for a fraudster; sometimes it's carried out by someone in order to buy a house they can't really afford and hence have to falsify documents. The key is to not get pulled into this sort of scam.

How does one cut down on real estate and mortgage fraud happening? Three steps:

1. Recognize it

2. Protect yourself from it

3. Report it

The most common scam is IDENTITY FRAUD leading up to Mortgage Fraud. In this type of scam, the fraudster steals the identity of the owner of a property so that they can sell or re-mortgage the property without the home owner's knowledge.

Steps you can take to prevent identity fraud are:

1. Obtain and verify the information in your credit report annually. Your credit report can be obtained through Equifax Canada or TransUnion Canada.

2. Shred or destroy all financial documents before throwing them out.

3. Review credit cards, bank and other financial statements on a regular basis.

4. Never give out personal information over the phone, email or online, unless you know who you're dealing with.

Common sense is your best asset against mortgage fraud. If someone is trying to get you to complete a real estate deal through dishonest means, or without giving you the information you need to make a decision, do not proceed.

Steps you can take to prevent mortgage fraud are:

1. Never sign blank documents that could later be filled with falsified information.

2. Never sign documents without fully reading them and understanding what they mean.

3. Never allow someone else to use your name and credit information in exchange for payment.

4. Never falsify information when applying for a mortgage, including overstating your income to get a mortgage that you can't really afford.

If you suspect that you or someone you know has been the victim of real estate fraud, please contact your local police department and the Real Estate Council of Ontario.

"Buying real estate is not only the best way, the quickest way, the safest way, but the only way to become wealthy."

— *Marshall Field*

Chapter 29: 7 costly mistakes to avoid when buying real estate

Home ownership is a big 'dream' for most of us. When you're getting ready to buy a home, there are many things to think about, prepare for and organize. Good preparation can make the difference between realizing that dream or getting a rude awakening through a costly mistake.

Here are 7 costly mistakes home buyers can make when purchasing a home:

Costly Mistake #1 - Not knowing what you can afford before making an offer?

The best way to avoid this is to go to a bank or mortgage broker and get pre-approved for a mortgage. How much home you can afford depends on how stable your finances are: what types of properties you're considering, the financing options available to you and how good your credit is. Usually pre-approvals are free. If thinking of making offers right away, being pre-approved for a loan will certainly help you in a bidding war to win that dream home. (*See Chapter 23: How much house can you afford?*)

Costly Mistake #2 - Choosing the wrong mortgage.

A bad mortgage can cost you thousands in interest. Shop for the best terms and conditions on a mortgage versus rate only. Check for the 3 P's - Penalties, Portability and Pre-payment Privileges. Consult your realtor or accountant before choosing the mortgage that's right for you. (*See Chapter 24: Shopping for a mortgage*)

Costly Mistake #3 - Not knowing who the real estate agent represents?

It is not advisable to share your seller's real estate agent. Unless the agent is working as *your* buyer representative, then assume that they in fact represent the seller. Many people don't realize this. Your buyer agent will represent your interests. The services are free and they are there to help you.

Costly Mistake #4 - Choosing the wrong realtor.

There are many realtors who are wrong for you. For example, the part-time agent who sells an occasional house because they need a little extra money or the insurance salesman who believes he can handle two careers. Getting an experienced, competent agent with your best interests in mind generally costs the same as hiring someone who is inexperienced. Bringing experience to bear on your transaction could mean a higher price at the negotiating table with minimum headaches. The person you select can make it a satisfying and profitable activity or a costly, terrible experience. It's your home, your money... make your selection wisely. *(See Chapter 4: Choosing an agent)*

Costly Mistake #5 - Not finding problems with the home before buying it.

You should always have a professional home inspector look at the home before buying it, otherwise you could be looking at huge repair costs later on. *(See Chapter 36: Home inspection–Do it! and Chapter 27: Buyer beware checklist)*

Costly Mistake #6 - Waiting too long to buy.

Although exceptions do occur, buying now nearly always proves wiser than buying later. When weighing the pros and cons of Renting versus Buying *(See Chapter 19: Buying versus renting)*, it pays to look into a variety of buying options even if you only plan to stay in the home a couple of years. Consider purchasing at bargain prices, buying a fixer upper where you can quickly create value, or buying a home that would make a good rental property investment *(See Chapter 32: Investing in real estate properties.)*

Costly Mistake #7 - Not knowing your rights and obligations.

Real estate law is extensive and complex. A purchase of agreement and sale is a legally binding contract. If improperly written, the contract can cause the sale to fall through or cost you thousands of dollars for repairs, inspections, taxes and remedies for items included or excluded in the offer. You must be clear and certain of the repairs and closing costs you are responsible for *(See Chapter 25: Hidden Closing Costs)*. You and your realtor must be aware of any defects or conflicts and how to remedy them to avoid losing money.

Chapter 30: How do you purchase a home that will appreciate in value?

If you're buying a new home, can you predict how well it will appreciate while you live there? Maybe so, maybe not.

People generally buy a primary residence as a place to live in and raise their families. Yet there are some things to look for in real estate that can help assure you that your property will increase in value over time.

Here are some real estate features that are likely to result in property appreciation:

Location, Location

A home's location will always have a huge impact on its ability to appreciate. Important aspects of location include school district rankings, access to parks, stores and restaurants. Transit, proximity of major highways and neighbourhood crime rates are also important considerations under location.

Keep in mind the principle of regression as well. By this I mean, don't buy the biggest house in an area surrounded by smaller homes. This will bring down the value of the bigger home, whereas the opposite is true for the smaller home in the area. Make sure the area conforms to and suits your needs.

Curb Appeal

A house that appears tidy and well-cared-for on the outside will sell more quickly and for more money. A good first appearance can add as much as 10 percent to the value of the home. This only makes sense, because if the exterior front of your house doesn't show well, buyers aren't enthused to check out the inside. Regular maintenance and upkeep of the front and back yard makes your property look good, contributes to the esthetics of the neighbourhood and shows you to be 'house proud.' Consequently, a messy overgrown yard not only gives a bad impression, but will need a great deal more time and money to clean up and eventually take longer to sell.

Upgrades and Repairs

Your home appreciates in value if it is updated and upgraded. You also want to save money by doing some of those upgrades yourself and over time. Timely fixes will help you enjoy your home while you live in it as well as grow your equity while it appreciates. (See *Chapter 7: Renovations that give the highest return*)

For Rental Properties

In order to maintain the appreciation value of a rental property, repair or fix all problems on an ongoing basis. Heating and plumbing problems, because of their unique nature, should be handled within 24 hours of learning of the issue. Other repairs and maintenance, including painting, floors, updating kitchens and washrooms, replacing appliances, window coverings and light fixtures will all help retain appreciation in value when the tenant moves out.

Tax Exemptions

Your 'principal residence' or residential property is generally tax exempt. Any gain or appreciation on the sale of a principal residence is tax-free. However, you should be aware that some tax rules do apply when selling your home. Investment properties or secondary homes are subject to capital gains tax. Your realtor will be able to guide you in this respect when you decide to sell your property. For the buyer, always assume you will need an additional 1.5 to 2.5 per cent of the purchase price to cover all closing costs.

Community Involvement

You may have a busy work and family schedule, but if you are able to be actively involved in your community and neighbourhood, you may be able to contribute to general upkeep and issues that concern the area. Studies have shown that when communities band together, crime rates, vandalism, vagrancy, littering, graffiti, and other anti-social behaviour is discouraged. Get to know your City councillor and make known your concerns.

Chapter 31: More single women are buying real estate – how and why?

It was not too long ago that a man used to handle all the finances in the home. In the last 10 to 15 years, there has been a significant shift in this status. It seems women are putting off marriage till later on in life, but they are not putting off what might be the largest single purchase of their life—a home. Gone are the days when women relied on men to support them and lay down the money for a home.

Women are marrying later, if marrying at all, and the high divorce rate has contributed towards this shift. Women's purchasing power is not just limited to condo living, because they are also buying homes and investment properties.

When I was 20, I bought my first condo apartment. I was young and single, but with the help of my parents I was proud at what I had been able to accomplish with my savings and on a single salary. If you're unsure about buying a home, talk to family and friends. Vent your concerns with them. Since these people know you best, they can help you decide the best course of action.

Never be afraid to ask too many questions of your realtor, mortgage broker, bank or lawyer. You need to be armed with the right information and understand the entire concept of buying and selling. Forget about feeling intimidated. Asking important questions gives you the control and the knowledge to make the right decisions.

Understanding mortgages - (See Section II–Shopping for a mortgage) You have got to be realistic about what you can and can't afford in a home. Think long-term. Consider what your life will look like in five or even 10 years. Don't stretch your budget too far and don't bite off more of a mortgage than you can chew. You want to be able to buy the home and still do what you want to do. Go to the bank, check your down payment and do your numbers and net sheet with your realtor. With interest rates and payments this low, you should be able to buy what you want and keep your mortgage payments low.

As a woman I know women want to have a friendly relationship with their real estate agent and/or mortgage broker. They don't want it to be just a transaction. Often buying a home is all about the transaction, but with most women, it is an intuitive process. It's all about the connection and the experience. It's important to get a sense of who you're working with and if they are a good fit before taking the plunge into buying a home.

Melanie, a divorced mom and nurse in her early 40's, called me about my condo listing that she had seen online. Unfortunately, that condo had a conditional offer on it. I explained to Melanie that I could arrange for her to view every other two-bedroom, two-bathroom condo in that building that was priced less than $350,000. There were five such properties up for sale.

I made appointments and we toured the five condos on a Saturday. She wanted to "think over" her decision. I called her on Sunday. She wanted to buy one of the condos we had seen but didn't "feel ready." By Monday it had sold!

Lucky for her, the following Wednesday, a price reduction popped up on one of the other condos she had seen and we made the offer that afternoon and she bought the home for full price! It was a little more expensive than the other one, but it was completely renovated with thousands of dollars in upgrades. Turns out it was identical to the condo on her Vision Board (*See Section III–Vision Boards*) with the added attraction of an amazing lake view. How's that for coincidence?

Later, Melanie called her mother to tell her the good news! She cried as we picked up her mom, her best friend and the kids as we all went to see it again. Everyone showered her with praise for finally making the move! Her parents were retiring and loved the area and asked me to find them a condo in the same location a few months later. The condo appreciated by 10% the following year. Everyone was happy!

If condos are not your thing, don't be scared to buy a house with an in-law suite, separate quarters or basement apartment. This gives you the option of renting out a room or parts of the house to a friend while at the same time sharing the expenses and getting help to offset your mortgage payments. Be sure to have proper leases in place when you are renting out even if it is on a month to month basis.

In some cases, you might even be interested in purchasing together with a friend to accumulate a bigger down payment by contributing equal portions, and qualifying for a higher mortgage by combining incomes. This can be tricky so make sure that you contact a lawyer to give you instructions and provide proper legal documentation when buying with a friend and/or especially with a group. Review title, all legal and binding implications on the contract.

There are many other special concerns and fears single women homebuyers have about buying property. If you're a woman who is considering buying a home on your own, and have a mix of eagerness and hesitation, then there are some considerations you should make note of.

- Securing a mortgage on one income

- Establishing a good credit score

- Start building your home buying team

- Check crime statistics in the area you are buying into. Go online to www. peelpolice.ca and click on the crime mapping feature.

- Visit schools and check school ratings online

As a woman purchasing a home or one who is experiencing a lifestyle change or one who is taking a big step into investment properties, you will still have many questions before taking the plunge into single home ownership. Whatever your reason for considering home ownership, this book should provide you information to help you in your research. You'll find info from: How do I begin? Who can I trust? How much house can I afford? Should I buy a condo? Should I buy a home with a secondary suite? Will I be able to afford the mortgage and other costs on my own? What type of mortgage should I get? How do I make an offer? Should I do an inspection? Renovate? Will I be safe there?

These questions and more are answered in this book, particularly in Sections I and II. I am hopeful that along with the answers, you will find useful tips and information! Happy reading!

Chapter 32: Investing in rental properties

Buying rental properties is the oldest and best way to increase your wealth. Investing in real estate has become increasingly popular and a common investment vehicle.

In most rental investment scenarios, an investor/buyer will purchase a property and lease it out to a tenant who then will indirectly pay part or all of the investor's mortgage and in some cases also property taxes by way of rental payments.

The owner/landlord is responsible for paying the mortgage, taxes and costs of maintaining the property. Ideally, the landlord charges the tenant enough rent to cover all of these costs. A landlord may also charge more in order to produce a monthly profit, but the most common strategy is to be patient and only charge enough rent to cover expenses until the mortgage has been paid down. Furthermore, the property will also appreciate in value over the course of the mortgage, leaving the landlord with a more valuable asset.

When investing in rental property, there is also the matter of finding the right property in the right location. You will want to pick an area where vacancy rates are low and choose a place that people will want to rent.

Here is an example of rental costs, income, expenses and profit:

Say you purchase a semi-detached house for $550,000.

You put a minimum of 20% as down payment to avoid CMHC insurance fees. That would be $110,000 – subtracted from the purchase cost, leaving you a balance of $440,000.

Always remember to keep extra money aside for Land Transfer Tax which equals $7,495 on a purchase price of $550,000 and around $2,500 for lawyers and moving costs. Approximate closing costs will be $9,995. Closing costs can also be added to your mortgage if there is lack of available funds.

Next you would need to arrange a mortgage with your bank for $440,000. A 5-year variable mortgage @2.9% with a 25-year amortization would equal approx. $1,937 a month for principal and interest plus the landlord/owner also pays the property taxes of $3,600 for the year (divided by 12 months equals $300 a month), which is then added to the monthly mortgage of $1,937 a month, which equals total monthly expenses of $2,237 a month. This is not including building insurance (which is approx. $600 for the year) plus repairs and miscellaneous.

The rent that the tenant pays is $2,200 a month plus utilities.

Rental expenses are $2,237 a month minus rental income which is $2,200 a month = Total rental expenses of $37.00 a month.

Rental income pays for the mortgage and expenses – less $37.

You will see from the above working and the investment calculation chart on the next page that the tenant is paying down the mortgage for your property. In addition, you also have pre-payment privileges on your mortgage at the end of each year, if you have extra savings and would like to put in a lump sum.

Another bonus is that the property appreciates at approximately 3% to 5% per year.

Your return on your appreciation is calculated:

3% of $550,000 (purchase price of the home)

= $16,500 times 5 years = $82,000 gross profit in appreciation

5% of $550,000 = $27,500 times 5 years = $137,500 gross profit in appreciation

In 5 years it is projected you will have made between $82,000 to $137,500 profit on your property. That is quite a substantial return on your investment.

On the following page is a chart that makes this calculation clear.

Investment Calculation		
Purchase Price:		$550,000
20% downpayment:	$110,000	
Land Transfer Tax:	$7,495	
Lawyers, misc:	$2,500	
Deductions:	$9,995	
Balance after deductions:	$440,000	
Owner gets mortgage		$440,000.00
[$440,000 - 5 yr Mortgage @ 2.39% - 25 yr Amortization]		
[Principal and Interest]	$1,937/month	
Taxes = $3,600/12 months	+$ 300/month	
Gross Rental Expenses	= $2,237/month	
(Building Insurance - $600.00 year + Repairs/Misc N/A)		
Tenant pays rent:		$2,200/month plus utilities
Rental Expenses:	$2,237/month	
Minus Rental Income:	$2,200/month	
		=-$37 month

- Rental income pays for mortgage & expenses
- Rent pays down your mortgage plus add yearly prepayment privileges
- Property appreciates approx. 3-5% per year

If you have less down payment and minimal funds, you can still get started purchasing rental properties. It is not easy, but it can be done. The main way is to buy the property as an owner-occupant and move into it and rent a portion of the home. After a few years, when you have built up equity, you can refinance the loan and move out, opening up the unit you've been living in to bring in even more cash flow. It requires patience and discipline but is a way that many rental property owners first get started.

Does investing in rental properties sound like something that might work for you?

Chapter 33: Second family units – in-law suites

Second family units, also known as basement apartments, secondary suites and in-law flats are self-contained residential units having kitchen and bathroom facilities with or without separate entrances within the structure of the same dwelling. Second units must comply with all applicable laws and standards. This includes the Building Code, the Fire Code and property standards bylaws.

Benefits of having second units

Affordability - Second units provide homeowners with an opportunity to earn additional income to help meet the costs of home ownership.

Help first time buyers get into the real estate market.

Support lifestyle changes, such as widowed/divorced and single income families.

Second units provide more housing options in changing demographics for *extended and growing families*, for example, a newborn, nanny's quarters, elderly parents, or a live-in caregiver.

Investment Payoff - Second units increase your investment portfolio by creating a nest egg. (*See Chapter 18: Real estate income–building a nest egg*)

Renovations increase value - You may need renovations to make areas of your home accessible to tenants or to accommodate your elderly parents, in-laws or adult children living at home. Finishing or renovating your basement or attic to create a second suite will definitely increase your home's resale value.

The pitfalls of second units

Impact on resale value - While many potential buyers will appreciate having a basement apartment that they too can reap the income benefits from, some may not like or want the same type of setup, which ends up reducing the interest and resale value of the home.

Repairs and maintenance - Every problem that your tenant has with the accommodation becomes your problem. There is no putting off a repair. You are now a landlord and have inherited this responsibility to your tenant.

Laws and regulations - Both landlords and tenants should be informed of the applicable rental laws in their province or city. Many of these laws if not followed can result in hefty fines.

Have a stranger in your home - Not only are there safety issues but you are now depending on someone else to pay you. Not all tenants are reliable, and it can be difficult to trust a stranger to hold up their end of the bargain.

Once you have weighed the pros and cons of having a second unit, make sure you know the difference between a legal and illegal basement suite. An illegal suite usually means that your home is not up to code. In this instance, be careful, someone may report you. Usually it is a neighbour or angry ex-tenant who does the reporting. The city may ask you to convert the unit to be up to code, or they may shut down your rental. Converting a suite into a legal suite can be very expensive. Besides that, you would also need to purchase an annual permit to maintain your legal suite–this doesn't cost very much ($50). The plus side is that it can look very official hanging on the wall!

Remember too, that many people who live in basement suites, do not want to live in suites that are mouldy, dark, and damp. Make sure there is sufficient light, heat, air ventilation and insulation between the basement suite and upstairs. Adding more carpeting and thicker underpadding within the basement rooms and on the upstairs floor can help decrease the sound transfer. Updated, renovated bathrooms and kitchens are very important to potential tenants. It's easy to figure this one out. Ask yourself: Would you want to live in it? Try your best to make your basement apartment as comfortable and liveable as possible and your tenants will be happy!

Chapter 34: Flipping homes—is it for you?

House flipping refers to buying a house, fixing it up and selling it for a profit in the same calendar year. Sounds easy, right? The logistics of doing so, however, can get pretty complicated. There are lots of decisions to be made before, through the process of buying and upgrading, to the sale of that updated property.

So with that in mind, if you're ready to put in the time and work, there is money to be made from flipping homes.

First step is to do the math.

- Figure out what you have to spend on the house, purchasing and renovation, down to the very last dollar.

- Price out the cost of carrying a short-term loan including the taxes, utilities and maintenance on the home for up to a year.

- Price out your material costs and labour.

- Look at comparable sales in the market to see what the likely sale price will be and don't expect a penny over.

- Every area has a not-to-exceed price. Don't over-price and don't over-improve. Keep your total budget within the sale price range.

Once you have a financial plan in front of you, with a reasonable margin for risk, begin shopping for homes that meet that budget.

- What should you buy?

- Where should you buy?

- How much should you improve the house?

Find a good house to flip in a geographic area you have fully researched, one that does not need expensive repairs. You should be able to buy the house for a low price, renovate it quickly and cheaply. Ensure that you personally supervise the repairs and make sure they are being carried out properly and on budget.

Flipping a house requires a lot of work and group of experts to be involved. A house flipper can certainly not go it alone. Start building your 'house flipping team' before you even start looking for homes. Your team at the very least should be composed of real estate brokers, contractors, architects, accountants and money lenders. All these professionals can help you shorten your learning curve and get you making money flipping houses faster than you would have been able to do on your own.

Speed equals profit. Time is of the essence. Speed is one of the biggest factors that will lead to profit. The shorter the time you hold onto your investment money, the better your profits will be. So make your improvements fast. Do the job well, but do it fast.

If all goes well, you could make a nice profit. But if something goes wrong, for example faulty budgeting, timing issues, a crime spike in that up-and-coming neighbourhood—you could be stuck with a house you can't get rid of and it will sit on the market for months.

Four house flopping mistakes:

1. *Not Enough Money* - Every dollar spent on interest and renovations adds to the amount you will need to earn on the sale just to break even and don't forget about capital gains taxes, which will chip away at your profit too.

2. *Not Enough Time* - It takes months to find a property, months to renovate, schedule inspections and meet building codes, months of meeting people at the property to sell it. If profits are not considerable enough, then it does not make sense and is not worth the time spent on flipping the property.

3. *Not Enough Skills* - The real money in house flipping comes from sweat equity. If you're handy, you have an advantage. On the other hand, if you have to pay a professional to do all the work, this reduces your investment profits drastically.

4. *Not enough knowledge* - Doing improper research without the help of a realtor. Trying to sell the home yourself to retain more profit could backfire. Realtors have the skills and training to be a great and useful ally in spotting the right property, helping with the area research and looking for buyers.

Use the **checklist** ☑ below to ensure that you focus on the most important and most profitable repairs for your **quick flip.**

Exterior (curb appeal)

☐ Do basic clean up and landscaping in front and back yards.

☐ Fill driveway and walkway cracks.

☐ Power-wash the siding, tuck-point a brick home, or paint a wood-sided home.

☐ Repair or replace windows, screens, shutters, front and rear storm doors, gutters (seamless are best), splash blocks and gutter extensions, exterior light fixtures, mailbox.

☐ Paint front door and garage including trim.

Interior

☐ Give the entire house a good scrubbing.

☐ Clean or replace drapes, blinds, doors/doorknobs.

☐ Remove hooks and nails and patch holes. Apply a fresh coat of paint to all rooms, using flat, neutral colors for the walls and semi-gloss white for the trim.

☐ Install new light switches and outlet cover plates, smoke detectors, thermostat, doorbell, register covers, exhaust fans/covers.

☐ Re-carpet, refinish, or replace damaged or worn flooring.

Kitchen

☐ Install new stainless steel sink, faucet, countertop (if worn), granite counter if possible.

☐ Refinish cabinets. Add new hardware.

Bathrooms

☐ Install new vanity and fixtures, toilet seat, towel hangers and shower curtains or install glass shower doors.

☐ Apply bead of caulk around the edges and base of tub, shower, sink, and toilet. Scrub grout between tiles.

Basement

☐ Whitewash concrete or cement-block walls with sealing paint. Paint the floor gray enamel.

☐ Install new glass block windows, if necessary.

☐ Buy a roll of insulation and stuff pieces of it between the joists and the outside wall. Dust off ductwork, pipes and wiring. Tack up dangling wires.

Mechanicals

☐ Clean or replace the hot water tank. Repair any leaky faucets. Unclog any plugged or slow drains.

☐ Change furnace filters. Check wiring, electric baseboard heating.

For more information that is relevant to flipping homes read *Chapter 7: Renovations that give the highest return.*

Flip Reno & Repair Formula
Here is the formula for a 'flip, reno and repair property':
MPP = Sales Price - Fixed Costs - Reno/Repair Costs = Projected Profit
<ul><li>MPP equals the maximum purchase price of Fixer Upper property.</li><li>Sales Price equals the conservative estimate of what you can sell the property for (not the price listed).</li><li>Fixed Costs equal all the costs, fees, and commissions that you can expect to pay during the project.</li><li>Reno/Repair Costs are the material and labour costs required to reno/repair the property into resale condition.</li><li>Projected Profit is the minimum amount of money you want to make off the project when it is complete.</li></ul>

The formula works like this: So if you buy a house for Maximum Purchase Price of $500,000 and sell it for—Sales Price of $700,000 minus fixed costs $50,000 minus Reno Costs $75,000 then the Projected Profit = $75,000.

Chapter 35: Are buyer assignments legal?

What is an Assignment? An assignment is a sales transaction where the original buyer of a property allows another buyer to take over the buyer's rights and obligations of the Agreement of Purchase and Sale, before the original buyer closes the deal. In other words, an assignment clause allows the buyer of a home to sell the place before they take possession of it.

In Ontario, assignments are more common in pre-built homes and condos than on re-sale properties, but they are possible on any type of trade.

You might well ask: Are assignments legal? When done properly, assignments are legal and can be a useful tool for buyers and sellers. For instance, someone could buy a condo that is still under construction and will not be ready to move into for a couple of years. If the buyer's work or family situation changes during that time, they may change their mind about living in the condo they have purchased. Another example may be where a buyer runs into financial difficulties at the time of close on an existing house and wants to find another buyer rather than risk the financial penalties in backing out of the deal. Assigning—if agreed to by the seller—allows the buyer to pass along the contract to another buyer.

What about the tax implications of assignments? The Real Estate Council of Ontario advises anyone participating in an assignment to seek the advice of a tax specialist. Generally, assignors can expect to pay tax on any profits they realized from the assignment. Land transfer taxes are paid by the assignee, as they are only due when the sale closes, that is the point when the property actually changes hands.

For an assignment to happen, the brokerage would have to inform the seller. The seller could then make an informed decision about whether to include an assignment clause in the agreement of purchase and sale.

Assignments can be a useful tool in some transactions. The seller's real estate representative is expected to help the seller weigh the pros and cons of giving the buyer the ability to assign the property to another buyer. Take enough time to review and research assignments in depth before making a clear decision if this is right for you.

REAL ESTATE & BEYOND

Chapter 36: Home inspection—Do one!

One of the most important things to do when buying a home is to get a qualified home inspection. Even if a house looks like a model home, we never know what is behind the walls, up in the roof, or underground till we have a home inspection. That said, be aware that some problems may go undetected even by a home inspector and may only make themselves known when they are eventually discovered.

Home inspections are primarily carried out by the buyer. However, it is not uncommon for the seller to have a pre-listing home inspection done so as to be aware of existing issues that can be fixed in a timely and cost-effective manner. The seller avoids the risk of buyers negotiating repairs off the asking price and gains the advantage of a move-in ready property that a buyer can buy with confidence.

How should a buyer or seller go about hiring or choosing a home inspector? The Canada Mortgage and Housing Corporation (CMHC) has a good resource base of professionals working in the housing industry. You could also ask your realtor who will have worked with many home inspectors and can recommend one.

Unfortunately, home inspection professionals are not regulated, nor do all have formal training, certification or insurance. Watch out for these 'non-professionals.' Be sure to interview two to three home inspectors before you decide. Ask for company name, certification and insurance.

Here are some of the common issues (and possible fixes) detected by a home inspection. Please use QUALIFIED electricians and plumbers, roofers, etc. for the safety of your property and yourself!

Outside the house:	
The Problem	The Cure
Poor grading and drainage—spongy soil around the foundation, signs of leaking in basement.	Regrade so that ground slopes away from the house. Remove porous material around foundations.
Faulty gutters, clogged or bent gutters, water not channeled away from house.	This should be on your preventive maintenance list. Make sure the gutters are of adequate size and splash pans are in place to divert run-off.

Roof problems—shingles are brittle or curled or broken or missing.	New shingle may have to be applied or worn/broken ones torn off. Replace flashings, especially around chimneys.
Poor upkeep of yard—fence/deck broken/shabby, cracked driveway.	Give the house an exterior face lift. For asphalt driveways use asphalt repair products to fill the cracks.

Inside the house:

The Problem	The Cure
Faulty plumbing—inadequate water pressure, slow drains, signs of leaks on ceilings.	Clean and route drains; reseat toilet with new wax ring, repair leaks.
Poor ventilation—extreme heat in attic, vapour condensation.	Ensure that roof soffits are not blocked; install additional roof vents; vent bathroom and kitchen fans outside.
Defective heating—cracks in the heat exchanger or water tank.	Reseal chimney flues; replace parts in water heater.

Basement:

The Problem	The Cure
Foundation flaws—cracks in foundation, sloping floors, sticking doors or windows.	Fill cracks with silicon caulking or epoxy; apply waterproof coating to the exterior.
Basement dampness—water stains, powdery residue on walls, mould or mildew.	Repair gutters to channel water away from house; apply waterproof coatings to basement.
Faulty wiring—this is a highly sensitive concern of buyers (and sellers as well) as it represents a fire hazard.	Junction boxes should be closed. There should not be any amperage mismatches. Get a qualified electrician to fix any problems and bump up the amperage to at least 100 amps.

A home inspector will detect mould in the attic and elsewhere, moisture penetration, faulty wiring and plumbing, pest activity, and much more. It makes sense to use a home inspector whether you are a buyer or a seller because you will have a better idea of what you are buying into or in the case of a seller, what you can fix in order to retain value on your property.

Chapter 37: How buyers can win a bidding war

It can be extremely frustrating for a buyer caught in a bidding war over a much-desired property. Multiple offers on your 'dream home' can be difficult to negotiate and come out with a winning bid. So what do you do? How far do you go to make it worth buying? There are some steps you can take as you step into a sellers' market looking to buy.

First of all, *get a solid loan approval*. Speak to your lender and get confirmed financing, so you are able to waive the loan approval condition in the sale requirement. Sellers prefer pre-approved finance offers which moves your bid to the top of the list.

Secondly, *shorten or waive some of the conditions in your offer*. Always get a home inspection, but try and shorten the time period when this is done. Try to get a pre-inspection of the home if there is time prior to making the offer.

Meet the seller's closing date. Don't ask for extra chattels or personal items. Keep the offer simple when in competition with other offers. The cleanest offer sometimes trumps the higher priced offer.

Next, *write your best offer*. Don't hope for negotiation or wiggle room in the price. Ask your agent for a Comparative Market Analysis to determine reasonable pricing. Sometimes sellers deliberately set a price below the comparable sales in an effort to generate multiple offers, so paying a little extra doesn't necessarily mean you are paying over market value.

Offer to *put down a large deposit when making your offer*. The deposit is part of your down payment. By increasing it above normal expectations, you are showing the seller you are serious about buying the home. It speaks volumes in terms of getting your offer moved up in the multiple bid war.

Know your limits. No matter how much you love the house, if it is just not worth the price, and especially if you cannot financially afford it in the long run, then it is better to walk away than be house poor or face serious financial consequences. Speak to a financial expert about worse case scenarios with your current income and savings. You should be doing this anyway when buying property, but especially so when you are competing in a bidding war.

A word of advice: if you already have a home and are looking to move to a new one, try to sell your existing home first. In a bidding war, if you are a first time buyer, renter or have already sold your home, you could have the advantage over a buyer who still needs to sell.

Sometimes buyers caught in a bidding war wonder if it's even worth trying to compete with multiple offers. With low inventory in the market, it is almost always a good idea to try. If you don't succeed, you can try again on another home or wait for inventory to increase so the buyer has more selection and less competition.

"Every person who invests in well-selected real estate in a growing section of a prosperous community adopts the surest and safest method of becoming independent, for real estate is the basis of wealth."

– Theodore Roosevelt

"A realtor is not a salesperson. They're a matchmaker.
They introduce people to homes,
until they fall in love with one.
Then they're a wedding planner."

– *Unknown*

SECTION III THE REALTOR

Chapter 38: Being successful in life

No matter how old you are, where you are from or what you do for a living, we all share something in common—a desire to be successful. However, each person's definition of success is different. Some may define success as being a loving spouse or a responsible parent, while most people would equate success with wealth and being financially independent.

There are a lot of tips and strategies out there on how to be successful in life, but I believe that there is no better way to succeed than to *follow the footsteps of a mentor*. A mentor doesn't always have to be a person you meet face-to-face. You can get access to successful mentors from the books or blogs you read.

Next, *find out what you love to do and do it!* You know you are on the road to success if you love what you do every day. Be confident and take action. Don't hold back from introducing new ideas in your way of doing and seeing things.

Don't be afraid of failure. Failure is simply the opportunity to begin again, this time doing something more intelligently. The truth is that we have to fail sometimes to succeed. So anytime we face failure, we should look at it as feedback and a way to succeed the next time we try. It is not a reason to give up.

Learn how to balance life. How you go about achieving balance in your life is the key to success. Pay attention to your health. We are far more productive and happier when we get enough sleep, eat healthy and fit in some type of activity or exercise into our routine.

Minimize toxins. By that I don't mean chemicals. Avoid the company of toxic people, the complainers, whiners, ones with poor attitudes. If you can't completely avoid them, at least minimize contact and tune them out as much as you can. Surround yourself with positive, supportive, can-do people whenever possible.

Set aside quality time with your family and friends. Don't just sit in front of the television. Have coffee with a friend, play a game with a child. Really get to know the people around you.

Always remember to have fun. Laugh, joke, play, find your sense of humour. Nothing makes you feel better than having a good laugh.

Always maintain a positive mental attitude. Have a razor focus on your goals. Don't let discouragement stop you from pressing on. Be brave enough to follow your intuition. Be willing to work hard and believe in your capacity to succeed!

My Success Chart!

I feel most successful when:

_____

_____

Times in the past I have felt most successful are:

_____

_____

To feel like my life has been a success I will need to accomplish:

_____

_____

An ideal successful day looks like this:

_____

_____

To my parents and others around me, I am judged successful if I:

_____

_____

My definition of success is:

_____

_____

Chapter 39: Keys to achieving your goals!

Every year, I see new real estate agents enter the business and I see many of them leave after a short time. Running a real estate business is not as easy, fun or glamourous as it seems. It involves a lot of hard work behind the scenes, many calls to clients and follow up, contracts and legal documents, abiding by strict rules and regulations, always being on call, working evenings and weekends, and dealing with emotional clients at an emotional time in their lives. Some 80% of new realtors leave the business within the first two to five years. That's right, 80%!

Here are 11 keys to keep you on the right track to achieving your goals:

- Key #1 *Positive Mind Set*: As with any career, you really ought to have the right mindset, and be keen on self-improvement and training. A good realtor never stops learning, improving their career knowledge base with ongoing training, being up-to-date on the latest technology and market trends. Doing this keeps them better able to serve their clients. The market is forever evolving and becoming more sophisticated. Demographics and lifestyles change and evolve, which means the average 'client' is changing in terms of needs and expectations. A good realtor works hard to stay abreast of changing times.

- Key #2 *Mentorship*: A new agent would do well to seek mentorship to gain from the experience and skills of senior staff and realtors. Sales skills are not something we are born with, but these can be honed by watching the pros, researching, reading success stories and just keeping ears and eyes open to what works and what doesn't. We all fear making mistakes, because they can be costly. But that said, bad experiences are learning experiences. A bad mistake can be a tough lesson never to be forgotten!

- Key #3 *Positive Attitude*: Keeping a positive attitude in a business like Real Estate, where there is lots of rejection takes work. Staying centered, on-track, and do your best in the circumstances that you are given. There are a number of recommended ways of staying positive. Many of these are freely available on the internet in books, webinars and podcasts. Try out the different options of meditation, yoga, power and rejuvenation breaks —

whatever you are comfortable with and see as a viable option for you. The point being to develop and maintain a sense of confidence and wellbeing, from which you will be better able to operate at your best.

☛ *Key #4 Being Confident:* If we are to be successful as realtors, then being confident, gaining the education and skills, staying sharp and focused and getting out of our comfort zone is a must if we want to achieve all our goals! Think out of the box, take those small risks, stand out and be different!

☛ *Key #5 Time management:* There is really no excuse for this. Whether you've come from a 9 to 5 job or straight out of school, or from a more laidback agency, you really need to quickly get into the habit of organizing your days and weeks to be as highly effective as you NEED to be in this demanding career. Whether in the office, on the road, showing properties, following up with clients, researching, attending open houses, networking, etcetera etcetera—you need to be on a day plan, a clear week plan, a marketing plan, and so on. Scheduled time for these work-related duties is crucial. If you have family commitments, work them into your schedule. Take advantage of driving time by listening to motivational real estate CDs when going to an appointment. Networking and camaraderie at the office is okay, but if it ends up eating up chunks of your in-office time with no benefits to anyone, then it is not helpful to you or your business. As months go by, if this is not addressed, it could lead to some very bad habits or even worse, an early exit from this amazing career!

☛ *Key #6 Prospect Consistently:* Realtors forget they need to *prospect each and every day.* Consistency is the key. Lead generation has to continue as an ongoing routine. What we prospect for now comes to fruition 30, 60 or 90 days down the road. The relationship you cultivate now, may not pay off for months and months. But by constantly adding new people to our database and keeping in touch regularly, we can expect to grow leads into deals and promote our own listings to a wider network.

☛ *Key #7 Follow Up and Communication:* You need to really *keep in touch* with your clients. I recently conducted a training program where I asked the class how often they get in touch with their clients in a year. I was shocked that some agents felt that 2 or 3 times a year was enough. A good agent will stay in contact between 12-24 times a year! Now I don't mean phoning each client that many times, but "touching" them that many times through helpful emails, birthday and holiday greetings, a monthly newsletter, personal notes, dropping off home show tickets and little gift cards, taking clients out for lunch, doing events such as family movie days, skating and swim days, client appreciation parties and more! All of these are excellent examples of how to stay in touch regularly!

☛ *Key #8 Spend Money on Marketing:* You need to *spend money on marketing!* This is not easy when you have already shelled out around $2000 for your license and board dues and the last thing you want to do is to spend more money! But, any good businessperson will tell you that you have to service your clients and in real estate that means you have to market their home. It is a proven fact that how much business you GET is directly correlated to how much you SPEND on marketing. You will receive many inbound leads when you establish a solid marketing campaign and get your profile out there as the go-to real estate agent.

☛ *Key #9 Be prepared for Appointments:* Agents who hustle into meetings, looking harried, shuffling loose papers in untidy folders, missing key information about the property they are showing their clients—do not exude confidence or professionalism. Quite the contrary! Having your listing presentation already prepared and practiced, complete with all required elements of statistics, market share, your bio, home marketing strategy and more is really important for you to make a good impression and show you are *the* realtor for the job!

☛ *Key #10 Internet/Video/Social Media Presence:* Become savvy with tech, web and social media. In today's business, it is crucial to build relationships and give helpful advice to your clients and online visitors through your website or by using social media. Use *video* to promote and sell your listings plus improve your *brand.* YouTube is a primary search engine. It keeps visitors on your website longer. Some people would rather watch a video than read an article. Videos also establish you as the expert. Provide ongoing communication and information through a blog or updates to your site. On average, people spend at least an hour on Facebook. Use targeted ads to reach potential clients on this forum.

☛ *Key #11 Keep in Touch with your Clients:* Don't forget about your clients! Even AFTER the sale. Far too often, real estate agents represent a buyer or seller just until the point where the transaction closes. Then they disappear never to be heard from again. That's a huge mistake, as the best time to foster client loyalty and prompt referrals from a satisfied client, is after the deal closes. Always treat your clients with the same intensity of interest and respect. You have helped them make one of the most important purchases they'll ever make and this can go beyond a business transaction to become a lasting relationship.

Goals:

Where in my life is my ambition healthy, with a positive driving force?

_____

_____

Where is my ambition maybe a bit **unhealthy**, jeopardizing more important areas of my life?

_____

_____

Do I love the destination I am travelling towards (my big goals)?

Yes? ☐   No? ☐

What are the biggest OBSTACLES I will encounter in achieving my big goals this year?

_____

_____

What will I do to continuously reinforce my passion and commitment to my goals?

_____

_____

What are my three absolute MUST ACHIEVE goals this year?

1. _____

2. _____

3. _____

Ten key items that can help you be more successful in your business and earn an EXTRA $50,000 to $100,000 in 12 months

1. Design and print a personal brochure

2. Develop a new Business Plan

3. Learn how to sell listed properties

4. Buy a lead generation program

5. Buy an automatic dialer

6. Hire a real estate coach

7. Join or start a team

8. Join a networking group

9. Focus on finding more buyer prospects

10. Buy a contact management system?

Chapter 40: The Pre-Game Preparation Plan

I.   Create your <u>business goals</u> first. Read them daily. Make sure they align with your <u>personal goals</u>.

1. Double my income from last year.
    Last year's income   This year's projected income

    _____

2. Incorporate two new systems.

    _____

    _____

3. Work on being consistent—it takes 21 days to develop a habit. Do the same thing consistently for 21 days.

4. Focus on only three things at a time and keep doing them routinely. For example: Calling past clients, wishing happy birthday, happy anniversary, giving home show tickets, giving regular market updates, asking for referrals.

5. Door knocking your geographical neighbourhood farm area, give business cards and invitations to your Open House.

6. Build a team and work less hours. Start with an admin assistant, then add field agents.

7. Fire yourself. Delegate what you are not good at, or free yourself up for what you are good at.

8. Keep in touch with my clients and build new relationships and referrals.

9. Tell everyone what your specific goals are for the year. Keep them posted on your progress—good or bad.

10. Read articles on adding value, different sales techniques, marketing plans, communication and improving services. Learn something new every day.

11. Write down three things that make you better than your competition, for example: track record and experience; knowledge of the area and/or live in the community; honest, reliable, regular follow up, keep in touch, etc.

_____

_____

_____

12. Ask yourself, what is the best realtor doing, that I'm not doing or that I could be doing better? Then do it!

_____

_____

_____

13. Be useful. Use your best hours to do your most valuable work. Shut the door for two or three hours. Work in solitude without interruptions.

14. Pick up the phone. Call your five best clients. Go visit them. Take them to lunch.

i)		Action:
ii)		Action:
iii)		Action:
iv)		Action:
v)		Action:

15. Organizing property open house events for agents and the general public.

16. Break up projects into smaller pieces. Start with something easy, then something harder, something easy, something hard, etc. till all tasks are completed.

Here's a handy chart to stick on your vision board (See next chapter):

Business/Sales Plan

Name: _____Date: _____

Designation:_____ Company: _____

My personal income goal for this year is $_____or $ _____ per mo.

I want to work _____ hours per week maximum.

I want to take _____ days' vacation this year.

Personal Production Goals

My volume and unit production goals for the next 12 months are:

	Sales Volume Goal	No. of Units	Commission
Month 1			
Month 2			
Month 3			
Month 4			
Month 5			
Month 6			
Month 7			
Month 8			
Month 9			
Month 10			
Month 11			
Month 12			
Totals			
Averages			

II. Create your personal goals. Read them daily.

1. Spend more quality time with family and friends.

2. Work at being healthy. Find out your optimum weight/BMI (body mass index)/blood pressure/cholesterol. Work at maintaining these optimum levels.

3. Be healthy: Drink a litre of water a day. Eat a healthy breakfast. Don't pick up junk food or fast food. Have a veggie and fruit or nut snack handy for energy. Watch your sugar and salt intake. Eat regular meals.

4. Exercise: Do the treadmill for 15-30 minutes at least twice a week. Workout with weights. Go to the gym if you need social motivation to stick to your routine. Have a game of tennis/squash. Swim if you can. Do yoga, spin or Zumba classes—whatever works for you—do it!

5. Enrich your spirituality. Read self-help books. Listen to inspirational and motivational audio when on the go or while doing house chores. Invest 15 mins everyday to watch motivational clips. Name three that you plan to listen to:

   Mine   *Yours*

   i. Tony Robbins   i._____

   ii. Robin Sharma   ii._____

   iii. Tom Ferry   iii._____

6. Be authentic versus plastic. Be kind and thoughtful. Do something nice for someone at least once a day.

7. Journal your thoughts and aspirations. Write down new ideas, small goals and practice positive affirmation.

8. Invest 15 minutes daily to plan your next day.

9. 'Me' time: Keep the last hour/half hour/15 minutes before bed to unwind. Meditate, give thanks, write in your gratitude journal, read or listen to music.

10. Travel: Plan short trips if you can't afford a vacation. Make sure you make time to relax and recharge.

11. Here's a handy chart on life goals to stick on your vision board (See next chapter on vision boards:

My Life Goals in 10 years:		
Career	Thinking ideally, how do I see myself earning a living in 10 years? In what ways is this allowing me to achieve my fullest potential?	
Health	In what physical shape do I view myself 10 years from now? What kind of exercise programs will stay with? How do I feel about my health?	
Family	What family relationships am I focusing on 10 years from now—what do those relationships look like?	
Spiritual	What does my spiritual life look like as I view it 10 years from now? What actions am I taking on a regular basis to enhance my spirituality?	
Social	What social activities will I engage in 10 years from now? What clubs or groups will I be actively involved in? Who are in my circle of friends?	
Financial	How much money will I need annually to support the above activities? Ten years from now, how satisfied will I be with my financial picture?	

Chapter 41: Action-Vision Boards—why you need them

Ready to take your business to the next level? Creating an action board can do that for you!

Have you heard of a vision board? A vision board is similar to an action board. You might want to try creating one. I have had vision/action boards for almost 10 years now. I have gone through three of them and am now on my fourth, which means that everything on my first three vision/action boards have manifested into my life through the Law of Attraction. Each goal on the boards has been accomplished and achieved!

Vision and action boards really do work! Every vision must be accompanied by an action plan. They can be created for personal goals and your business goals. When you start off, it is simpler to have one board for personal goals and another for business goals. It is easier to concentrate and focus on one board at a time.

The vision/action board should be prominently placed in your home or office where you can focus on it. Keep a picture of it on your phone so you can look at it and have it with you at all times. For real estate agents, this can be a very powerful tool to reach your goals in business and in life.

Creating a vision/action board couldn't be easier: Start by getting in touch with your inner child. All you need is a large piece of poster board, magazines, scissors and glue, and you can cut and paste to your heart's content!

First, let's get clear on "why" we want to create a vision/action board! The law or rule of thumb is:

- When we focus all our attention on something, we are going to experience more of it!

- Selectively paying attention to these things that we want to achieve, will intensify the feeling and put more focus on them!

- When you focus on the vision you want to create, you won't even notice the obstacles, which makes you take action quickly and confidently.

- It literally transforms your thinking. It helps you clarify your dreams and intention and gives you a visual reflection of your goals and a plan of action.

To prove that vision/action boards work, I set out to try an experiment that I had read about. The first day I focused on red cars all day. That day I saw over 300 red cars. I said to myself this is too easy. Next day, I went out and focused my attention on lime green cars. More difficult, right? How many lime green cars do you see? In the first 10 minutes I saw a lime green tractor trailer truck zooming down the highway; 15 minutes later I saw another lime green truck turning at the lights. Then I saw three lime green cars in a retail store parking lot! All in the first hour. Truth! Amazing! You should try it and see what happens!

What you think of, each day, is what you attract. Everything in life, good or bad, is manifested by you! What you surround yourself with, is what you become. And that is basically how vision boards work.

When creating a vision/action board:

1. Decide what it is you are trying to attract: This may sound easy but a lot of people have trouble with this. So let's figure it out by thinking the reverse. Figure out what are the things that you don't want in your life. When you know what you don't want, it can help clarify what you do.

2. Go through magazines and tear or cut out all the images and words that 'speak' to you or resonate with you. These images and words should fit the categories you've decided to focus on and should feel in alignment with your goals and dreams. Organize all images and apply.

   Don't just randomly pick a photo! Take the time to be specific about precisely what it is you are after. If it's a dollar amount, make sure you are clear about what that amount is. Some other ideas are:

   • Exceed sales goals every month
   • 100 new contacts each quarter.
   • Annual revenue exceeding $1 million.
   • What your desired office space might look like.
   • Types of clients or customers you want to attract.

3. Feel it, don't just think your way through the exercise. Make sure it is a true action board as well. Don't just include the pictures of the outcome. Include the where, what, when, and why, and how this will occur. Visualization coupled with an action plan will get you closer to your goals and dreams faster. When you're finished, hang it up and engage.

How do you *engage* is the next question? What are things that can get in the way of creating a positive and effective outcome from your vision/action board?

- Your beliefs are in conflict with your goals. Saying you want something but not believing you actually deserve it.

- Not really caring about it. Putting more interest in what others want from you instead of what you desire yourself.

- Faking it! Doubting it will work. Practicing till you make it. Without making authentic connections, what do you think you will attract?

- Not seeing results quickly enough and giving up on your dreams.

Following is an action plan that can be used to complement and implement your vision/action board goals.

	TOP 10 IDEAS COLLECTED TODAY	F E P
1.		
2.		
3.		
4.		
5.		
6.		
7.		
8.		
9.		
10.		

F=*Fast,* **E**=*Easy,* **P**=*Profitable*

If I implemented every one of the ideas above into my real estate business practices, I estimate my income would go up $_____.

From the above, these are the **top three** ideas and my **next plan of action**:

1. _____

Plan of action_____

2. _____

Plan of action_____

3. _____

Plan of action_____

Tips: Take each idea above and write it down on separate 3" x 5" cards. Implement one at a time. Once mastered, select the next one, do the same to implement. Next, voice-record the best ideas you collected and listen to your recording 3-4 times a week for the next 30 days. Believe me, it is incredibly effective. It works!

Chapter 42: Build Connections—Create Instant Rapport!

Creating instant rapport with the people you meet in your life is one of the most important business (and personal) skills you can acquire. Your ability to create rapport helps you build friendships, boost your business and makes your clients feel comfortable so they can trust and relate to you. Here are some effective tips for creating instant rapport:

1. *Begin the interaction with a SMILE.* Smiles are infectious. TRY IT. Smile at yourself in the mirror. Look directly in people's eyes, shake their hands and smile. Have an open mind, a positive attitude, and make an effort to find a connection.

2. *Address people by their names.* People love the sound of their names. This builds rapport and familiarity, and is like talking to a friend. However, don't overdue it. Make it natural, not forced. It can be difficult to remember the names of everyone you meet. In the real estate business, you constantly meet so many people. Here are five ways to remember names:

   • Repeat their names twice after you first hear it, for example, say Sophia, Sophia

   • Create a rhyme or 'sounds like'—on the sofa, Sophia

   • Relate the name to someone famous—Sophia Loren

   • Find a feature you can relate their name to—sophisticated Sophia

   • Ask them how to spell their name—Sophia or Sofia

3. *Open up the conversation.* Comment on something you see, hear or feel in the environment. Ask a question that relates to that observation and their views on it. Reveal something about yourself to relate to what they've said. Here are six really easy useful questions:

   • How did you get started...?

   • What advice would you give...?

   • Who has most influenced you...?

   • Why did you get involved in...?

   • Where do you think...?

   • When do you see this happening ...?

   There are no perfect opening questions! Try to read the situation and go with it. Just be yourself.

4. *Listen with full attention.* Notice when you have stopped listening and refocus yourself. People have a sense of knowing when you're distracted and are not listening. Make sure you are looking at them and not your phone or around the room and nod attentively.

5. An integral part of building rapport is the technique of *matching and mirroring.* Match their posture, facial expressions and gestures. Make the person feel valued. Pay real attention. Studies at the University of Pennsylvania have shown that only 7% of building rapport with people comes from the actual meaning of the words we speak. The other 93% of rapport comes from matching and mirroring the other person's behavior.

   - *Matching and mirroring their voice.* In real estate, your voice plays an important part in building rapport with clients and prospects. Apart from face to face appointments, the majority of your time is spent on the phone. During these phone calls, your voice is the only tool you have in making people feel comfortable and feel that you are definitely the best person to work with.

   - *Focus on matching the volume of their voice.* Except of course if they are angry and loud. Then your own tone should be progressively quieter and controlled.

   - *Pace yourself at the same tempo.* Don't ramble on if they are talking slowly. Give them time to speak. Listen attentively, not impatiently.

   - *If they talk quick and on point, you be clear and on point.* Don't stumble and hesitate. Speak clearly, pausing to see if they are following your line of thought.

6. *Don't cross your arms when speaking to someone.* This may not seem like a big deal, but crossing your arms represents a sign of defense or closing up. Best to leave your hands by your side.

7. *Choose your attitude.* Your attitude always precedes you especially in face to face interactions.

Connecting with people may seem so difficult, but if you follow these simple rules you will see your business increase substantially. You will instantly build rapport and make more lasting connections.

Fill in Chart II.42, which will help you evaluate your recent business, personal and social connections. Then expand your list by building instant rapport with new connections.

Chart II.42: My Business, Personal and Social Connections

Professional	L/D/E	Personal	L/D/E	Social	L/D/E
1.		1.		1.	
2.		2.		2.	
3.		3.		3.	
4.		4.		4.	
5.		5.		5.	
My New List		My New List		My New List	
1.		1.		1.	
2.		2.		2.	
3.		3.		3.	

L=*Limit Association,* D=*Disassociate,* E=*Expand Association*

Chapter 43: Asking for Referrals—when, where, how?

Asking for referrals is probably one of the most important activities you can do to keep your business pipeline in continuous flow. But it's sometimes one of the hardest things for real estate agents to do.

Your approach regarding referrals is what makes all the difference. Dale Carnegie noted that 91 percent of customers say they would give referrals. Yet, only 11 percent of salespeople ask for them.

Most realtors don't want their client to feel uncomfortable or impose on them so they don't even pose the question of a referral. Others only gently hint at potential business contacts.

Here are some 'scripts' you may want to reword your queries for referrals:

- *"If you have any friends or family who would be interested in buying or selling, I hope you will pass out my business card."* This is still too subtle. You're almost assuming the client has no family or friends! A better technique to use when asking for referrals is to say:

- *"Here are five of my cards, please hand them out to your family and friends who might be interested in our services."* If the client accepts the cards, odds are slim they will remember to hand them out. In addition, this is a statement, not a question. It is better to ask a question and get a verbal commitment. For example: *"Will you please hand out my cards...?"* The client is obliged to say 'Yes' and will likely do this for you. But ask yourself, what do you really want to happen? You want the names and contact details of people who want to sell or buy a house. Even if you're shy by nature, write down and practice all the scripts and then try asking this.

- *"Since you are happy with my services, would you please introduce me to someone you know who is thinking of buying or selling soon?"* A satisfied client will give you actual leads or even bring in a prospect to make the introduction. It doesn't get any better than this. Try it. See what happens. Then follow up with a show of interest in the referrals that the client comes up with. Thank them and say you will get back to them.

The Rule of Reciprocity

There are other ways to get referrals. Have you heard of "The Rule of Reciprocity"—the practice of exchanging things with others for mutual benefit? When someone does something for us first, we are more likely to respond positively to them.

There are many ways that you can use this technique to get more referrals.

- Provide referrals to a contractor, lawyer, lawn maintenance, accountant, interior decorator or other resources—and watch them give back.

- Give a potential referrer a special gift, share a recipe, offer business advice, take them out for dinner or lunch. They will return the favour.

- Try these suggestions, then always follow up with a phone call and ask for the referral.

When should you ask for referrals?

Ask your client for the referral 3-5 times over the selling process:

- During the listing interview, after you have sold them on your exceptional service, when the client is comfortable and happy to move forward, you could get them thinking about referrals: *"I don't make my living off any one transaction. I make my living off of your referral business. If you are pleased with my service, will you refer me to your family and friends?"*

- During the sales process, once the customer is starting to see the results. An example: *"I am glad that everything is working out so well. Now that you understand how we work and the systems we use, we could really use your help in referring us to other people who want to buy or sell a home. Do you know of anyone that may be in need of my services?"*

- Just after the closing, once the transaction is complete and they are greatly appreciative. An example: *"Working with you was a pleasure, and it's important to me to make sure that you have been happy with my service. I am proud of our high rates of customer satisfaction. How would you rate my service to you?"* (wait for answer). *"If you have friends, relatives, or associates who need real estate assistance, would you feel comfortable referring me? Do you know of anyone I should be talking to right now?"*

- Post-sale follow-up makes good business sense. It lets customers know you are interested in their wellbeing and makes it easy to ask for referrals later on. Ten days after the closing, call to say: *"Hello, it's Carmela calling. How did the move go? Is there anything more I can help you with? I'll check in with you again in a month."* Then, in a month, call again. This time, ask for referrals, saying: *"I know we did a great job for you, and I'm hoping you will refer us to your new neighbours and work associates. Do you know of anyone who is planning to buy or sell a home?"*

Another way of obtaining referrals is from your personal service providers. Here are some people you should get to know:

- *The florist.* They assist with weddings and funerals and send bouquets that celebrate new arrivals. They know people who are making life transitions.

- *The hairdresser or nail technician.* I get my nails done every week with the same woman, and no one has sent more business my way. It's important to be a loyal patron and they are likely to be loyal to *you.*

- *Schools and PTA.* I've received a lot of business through contacts I've made at my children's schools. I've found that most of my relocating buyers came from referrals from the Parent Teacher Association.

- *Wedding Planner.* Last year I did a bridal show and connected with a wedding planner. This is an ideal way to find first time buyers.

- *Bank Managers.* Sometimes buyers/sellers don't have a realtor and will ask their bank consultants to recommend a real estate specialist in the area when getting pre-qualified for a mortgage.

- *Neighbourhood/place of worship events.* Sponsor an ad or booth or stall—establish a presence in your area events or local newsletter/bulletin.

Follow this information and these referral scripts consistently and you will see great results. Your business will improve tenfold! Good luck!

Chapter 44: Thank you notes

It may seem old fashioned, but the magic of a thank you card—the kind you actually drop in the mail—really works! I made a habit of using thank you cards and it has helped double my productivity! The reason behind this is that thank you notes do the right thing at the right time with the right intention.

- People who receive it, actually read it
- They keep the card for a period of time
- Perhaps even post it on their fridge or special place

Thank you cards or notes are effective because it isn't a popular form of communication. How many thank you cards have you received in the mail this month?

Let me tell you a story about the power of thank you cards. This is something that happened to me.

About five years ago, I called someone in my area who was selling a house privately and asked if I could help them sell their home. He told me to come and have a look. I went over to view the home. He asked me to "Show it if I had a buyer."

A week later I followed up with a call. He said "Guess what? I sold it!" I said "Congratulations! Good luck! Then I quickly sent him a thank you note to thank him for letting me see the house and considering my services."

The day when he received the Thank You card, he was at his lawyer's office and he met another person who was in the process of a divorce and who asked him if he knew any good real estate agents. **Guess who's name he gave him?** The 'private for sale' guy called me to tell me he passed on my name. The guy from the lawyer's office called me to set up an appointment that same night. I listed his home the next day with the co-operation of his ex-wife. The house sold in three days. I ended up selling him a condo and his ex-wife a townhouse. His ex-wife had a younger sister working downtown who was looking to buy her first condo. That month I found her the perfect condo downtown. Everyone was pleased and happy! All this came about with one Thank You note and four transactions later.

When you touch another person in a special way and show them you care, whether there is financial gain for you or not, incredible things happen. We are not just in the real estate business. We are in the people-caring business.

Here are other ways you can say "Thanks" with a card:

- When a client or other referral source gives you a referral.

- When a prospect calls you to do a market evaluation and explain your service. For example: Thank you for having me over to meet you and your family...

- When a client asks you to recommend a contractor, lawyer, stager or other home professional. For example: Thank you for putting your trust in me...

- When you talk on the phone to someone who is thinking of selling in three to nine months or a year. For example: Thank you. It was a pleasure speaking to you on the phone about your plans for moving...

- When a client attends your client appreciation event.

- When a client has been great to work with (hopefully that's all of them!)

- When you enjoyed spending time with someone or meet a person you would like to get to know better.

- When you receive a gift or give a person a gift.

Other special cards you can send are birthday cards, anniversary cards, 1st year, 5 years, 10 years in client's new home, newborn baby, baptism, wedding and the list goes on.

You can also send thank you notes to Expiry's, FSBO's, lawyers, bankers, home stagers, cleaning services, movers, your colleagues and just about everyone you do business with. It keeps your name in the forefront of their mind when it comes to referral business.

Don't be tempted to send a cookie-cutter card. It will come across as insincere. Take the time to write a personal message, in your own handwriting. This will be time well-spent and will be remembered and appreciated!

Chapter 45: Open houses! Generate more sales!

The goal of an open house is first and foremost to sell your client's home. When you find a buyer and make the sale on your client's behalf, you will not only have generated more income, but you now have a satisfied client who will be pleased to refer you to their neighbours, friends and family. The secondary goal is to attract new prospects and brand yourself as the Neighbourhood Real Estate Expert!

Open houses have changed over time due to the rise of the digital age, which now sees 80% of real estate leads coming from the internet. So now, once you've brought in the leads, the key is to get those people away from the computer and establish face-to-face connections so that you can build and make the relationships stronger. One way to have personal interaction is to host what I call "themed and branded open house community events," inviting your prospects to view the home if they are interested and get to know you on a personal level.

What is the single biggest mistake agents make when hosting an open house?

There isn't one single mistake that most agents make, rather it is a series or combinations of mistakes that result in an unsuccessful open house. One mistake agents make when it comes to open houses is that they 'wing it' and as a result, they are unable to generate high demand from their open houses.

However, they can improve their results by doing the following:

- Marketing and promoting the open house during the week leading up to the open house. For example: send out personal invites, flyers, postcards, and go to local businesses in the area and invite them to co-promote your open house. They'll be happy to leverage this opportunity to expand their own brand.

- Educate yourself extensively about the neighbourhood so that you can offer a unique value proposition to the buyer or seller leads that walk into the open house.

- Use numerous open house signs (I recommend 20-100 signs or sandwich boards). If you have a team and are able to do 2, 3 or 4 open houses that day/weekend, the multiple signage integrates all the open houses together for more powerful marketing and brand recognition. Make sure to get the signs out a few hours before the open house.

- Conduct the open house properly. This includes staging and showing the house, keeping track and order of visitors, and asking key questions to determine how ready the lead is to book an appointment.

- Engage with visitors as they come through the door - introduce yourself, offer them a brochure, give them your business card, take them for a tour of the house and be friendly.

- Get the open house attendees to share their information with you for future relationships. This information can be used for you to follow up on the visit to the open house and assist them with any further real estate information.

- To encourage people to submit their correct information and provide feedback on the open house, ask them to sign in with their email on your laptop or enter heir name in a draw for a gift basket or gift certificate, free market evaluation, free staging, etc.

- Always make sure to follow up immediately with the leads that visited your open house and keep close touch with them by phone or through email. Set them up on a CRM system to receive real estate information and updates.

Some important steps for hosting an open house

1. For you, the agent, to select the right property. Make sure the house is reasonably priced, staged, and located in a popular neighbourhood.

2. Make sure the seller is in full cooperation with the ultimate open house event coordinated and designed to gain maximum exposure to the many guest attendees and potential buyers that come through.

3. Pre-open house preparation: ideally you want to begin marketing the open house about 5-7 days before if you are placing flyers throughout the neighbourhood, direct mail, door knocking or phone canvassing to invite people.

4. Provide unique and personable experiences during the site visit to the customers so that everyone feels comfortable, can envision themselves in the home, and can ask important questions that will ultimately lead to an offer.

5. Recall the value of your brand and property. During the open house, you will be seen as an expert in your area. Know every property that sold, is listed, is coming up for sale and didn't sell. Know the schools, transit

routes, community centers, shops, demographics, etc. of the immediate area.

6. Follow up right after the open house and in the weeks following the open house. You can send surveys allowing visitors to rate their motivation and satisfaction. You can extend the campaign beyond 6-12 months, so you continue to learn and adjust your business while maintaining a relationship with clients and prospects.

Create a marketing plan leading up to the open house.

The marketing strategy and daily presentation leading up to the open house is crucial in determining the number of people that attend your open house and also the number of buyer/seller leads you generate.

Keep these points in mind:

- Make sure you are getting out there and knocking on the doors of about 100 homes to the left and 100 homes to the right of your upcoming open house.

- Put an open house rider on your 'For Sale' sign 5 days before your open house. This helps bring more people to the open house.

- Place ads in the newspaper, send direct mail invites, call your database and invite previous open house attendees to help increase attendance at your open house.

- Push the open house event on social media (Facebook, LinkedIn, Twitter, YouTube video), on your website and blog. Also make a landing page on Kijiji or Craigslist to significantly increase the reach for acquiring new buyers and sellers to your open house.

Turn your open house into a true event! Make it theme-based or holiday-based. Make it stand out and be well attended.

Set up 8 ft. agency balloons in front of the open house to attract people in the area to join the event. Put coloured balloons on your open house signs around the neighbourhood. Offer incentives to reel the guests in early. Try to create theme-based open houses to significantly boost attendees.

Along with the themes, have giveaway bags that include branded material. We usually give out our 8-page branded real estate newspaper that displays our bio, all our listings for sale in the area, mortgage sheets and colour brochures prepared for the open house property and an info sheet with schools/neighbourhood amenities. Some treats and goodies, gift certificates and household tips and treasures. This ensures that attendees leave with added value to their open house experience.

Here are some themes to consider:

- *Halloween theme:* Give pumpkins to the first 10 families, and candy loot bags, chips or Cheetos to kids, pumpkin cookies, and coffee/apple cider for adults.

- *Easter theme:* Give Easter lily plants to the first 5-10 families, and chocolate loot bags to kids.

- *Wine & Cheese theme:* Host a wine basket draw giveaway, and offer wine tasting from a 'make your own wine' store (including coupons and discounts).

- *The Guest Connect theme:* Give clipboards to rate each room, the house exterior, basement, and price - which provides info for the seller and the agent. Provide small gifts to those that participate.

- *Garage Sale theme:* Encourage clients to have a garage sale at the same time as the open house to attract more people. This helps them make some money while de-cluttering their home, and trying to sell their home at the same time.

- *Summer BBQ theme:* Park a cart in the driveway acting as a hot dog stand, ice cream cart (rent) and get a friend or family member to man it in order to save time.

- *Spotlight Local Businesses in the area:* This will attract attention to your open house while doing the good deed of showcasing a local restaurant (who in turn will help promote your event). You will supply food, drinks or samples at the open house and also get extended exposure. People love free food and it shows you as a supporter of the local community. It brands you as the specialist in the area.

Get open house visitors to sign-in

Visitors are sometimes hesitant to sign or leave correct information. To ease the anxiety, explain that it is our security and safety requirement to protect our seller/buyer. Visitors would understand that if it were their home, they too would want their realtor to follow this security requirement.

In addition, we try to make it fun by offering them a chance to win something like lottery tickets, restaurant gift certificates, sports tickets, a wine basket and other gift baskets - even gingerbread houses during the Christmas season. People love the opportunity to win gifts so they will fill in correct information.

Some of the questions we ask our visitors are:

* Are you working with an agent?
* Have you signed a Buyer Representative Agreement?
* Are you thinking of buying or selling this year?
* Would you like a Free Home Market Evaluation?
* Would you like to be contacted by phone – email – neither.

Sign-ins can be digital on your laptop (Open House Pro) or hard copy. After the open house, follow up with all your visitors through a digital CRM tool like Top Producer, Boomtown, or Tiger Lead.

Once you gather the contact information (and assuming they checked off that they wish to be contacted), then you would add them to your database and separate them into categories being: A - Hot lead, B - Warm lead, C - Cold lead and then again by sub category of Buyers, Sellers, Prospects.

For buyers, you would send them homes that you think they would like to view that matches their criteria and price range.

For sellers, you would send them reports on selling their homes and comparable properties that are for sale in their neighbourhood.

You can send *both buyers and sellers* quarterly newsletters to keep in touch and seasonal postcards as well as birthday and anniversary cards. This will help you begin to develop a relationship with them and become the real estate agent of their choice.

Final word on open houses!

Always have at least two agents doing the open house together – not only for safety reasons but also to service the open house attendees' needs and answer questions promptly. It is a priority to keep order so you can qualify the buyers and make an appointment with them during the open house. In order to appropriately pay attention to every prospect, I'd suggest not allowing more than 2 or 3 families to be in the home at the same time. Let people wait outside for a few minutes before letting them enter the house. This way you can make sure that every visitor has a great time during your open house.

Bonus reminders!

- Remember that the same old thinking will give you the same results!
- Have a positive mindset and change your attitude!
- Think outside the box and have a successful open house!

An open house can **ultimate brand** you and help you become more than just a salesperson! The way to improve your brand is by studying and marketing the area thoroughly, knowing everything and everyone within the community. Co-marketing with local businesses in the area, creating referral partners and a greater introduction to you, the realtor, and to the open house community. Internet branding can display this further through your website, video blogs, social media, YouTube, Trulia, Zillow, Kijiji, Craigslist and much more (see other chapters).

Plus, promoting your brand over your geographical farm area through bi-monthly mailings, as well as institutional marketing such as billboards, bus shelters, bus wraps, bus benches, car wraps, etc. can super increase branding exposure.

Last, but definitely not the least, farming individual open house areas with unique themed out-of-the-box, well-planned open house events alongside multiple-area signage (from 20-100 branded signs) for maximum results and **ultimate real estate branding!**

The Conversion Strategy						
	# Open Houses per Weekend	# Open Houses per Month	# Guests per Open House	# Families per Open House	# Families (Contacts) per Month	Sales per Month @ 0.01% CR
Team	4	16	30-90	10-30	160-480	2-5
Individual	2	8	30-90	10-30	80-240	1-3

*Average 3 guests per family. Sales calculated at a 0.01% Closing Rate multiplied by the number of Contacts.

Chapter 46: TV and media advertising—how it works

Television dominates all other advertising media. It is the most forward thinking nuance marketing method in real estate today and is the most advanced ultimate branding. Television educates viewers in a highly "visual" manner through entertainment. The real estate industry uses this medium to impart useful information on the latest trends in business and features properties available on the market.

For the realtor, television is said to "accelerate and differentiate" you and your business from the numerous real estate agents practicing in the residential housing market today. This is a choice medium for innovative entrepreneurs who intend to take their business to the next level. It raises your profile as a cut above the rest.

Most of you think that television, radio and video are very expensive media to venture into and rightly so. In most cases it is, but let me relate my own story of how I got involved in television. I hope it inspires you to consider doing the same.

I have spent almost three decades of my life in the real estate business. I have learnt a lot and for the longest time, I've been determined to bring about much overdue change in the industry. I wanted to step out of the routine methods of doing business and contribute to change in the industry–giving back to the profession that has brought me such career satisfaction.

Here is how my journey to having my own television show progressed:

Firstly, I started a special networking group and organized networking events, which were highly appreciated by members. I invited renowned political and community speakers to address the group. I was chairman and CEO of the group.

In the next step forward, I founded an organization and moderated groups in round-table panel discussions at landmark city and community developments, bringing awareness and attracting business to those establishments and events. In collaboration with select guest panel speakers, we coached participants in real estate issues as well as life issues in general. Audience feedback was amazing and we had requests for audio and video copies of the events.

Greatly encouraged by these requests, I hired a film crew to produce not only a video, but a high quality program that would open up our live events to the internet viewers–hence multiplying the numbers benefiting from the program. Our live audience online network Real Estate TV Show was born!! It was called *Kapeleris Talk TV - Real Estate & Beyond.*

I was the producer and TV host of the show and hired an assistant producer, director, lighting and technical specialist, a two-man camera crew, editor and videographer. There were many volunteers who contributed their time behind the scenes and wanted to be a part of this exciting, innovative, in-demand new concept.

As well, I had to select a name and logo that simultaneously progressed the continuum of our brand and emphasized what the theme and TV show was about.

Next step was to hire a musical producer and technician to come up with an original theme song and original show introduction.

Next, create a social media Facebook page, fan page, group page and boot it up with LinkedIn, Twitter, Google+, Instagram and ultimately YouTube.

Our website and Evite boosted the live audience and attendance to the show created a buzz and immediate interactive marketing response.

Note: The Online TV show never stayed stationary or was it filmed in a studio. The show continued to move from one part of the city to another. It was filmed in hotels, restaurants and business establishments of all kinds. With this method, a greater live audience was captured which propelled greater word of mouth recommendations in terms of Real Estate referral business (based on the benchmark we were setting for our industry)

Of course, this was slightly more expensive and if your objective is to be cost-effective, then you may want to start taping from your office or rent a small studio.

I want to bring to your attention that, as glamorous as television is and as glamorous as you think it may sound... I can truly say... it was the most contrecoup, demanding, laborious and challenging project that I have ever initiated.

With perseverance and steadfast determination, it became also the most exhilarating and lucrative project that I ever accomplished. Tenacity and passion for the work is what is required to see it through.

Then things got even better! Rogers Cable TV Studios noticed the brilliant marketing and lively animated TV productions with stimulating moderated discussions and fascinating guests from our YouTube TV Video Station and asked if they could repurpose the videos on Cable TV to a wider distribution network. Further, in collaboration, we produced 23 more new cable TV shows for the studio while the show still airs today and we continue to grow strong on our journey to provide key information and value to a general audience.

Television dominates all other advertising media. Whether you are making your first TV commercial or looking to create your own Real Estate TV show, you'll want to achieve results that raise your brand awareness, boost sales, generate more leads and define you as "The Expert."

If you are creating a commercial for television, keep this in mind:

- viewer retention is rated at only 20, 30 or 60 seconds
- avoid cramming too much in a short space of time
- evaluate the script, read it out loud
- check it for timing and accuracy
- does it flow well and present the key message

The most effective commercials have a hook—they set up a situation or problem and present a solution followed by a call to action.

If you are creating a TV show, you need to first consider:

- who is your audience?
- the demographics and the distribution area
- what questions does the average client need answered?
- what is the best way to communicate with the client?
- what is the focus of the show?
- what type of show would get the best response?

In order to achieve high quality without a big investment in time from you, you may want to get a production company to produce the show for you. If that is the case, you will need to discuss your brief with them, agree on a creative direction, budget and timescale.

TV remains the most effective marketing tool for advertisers, boasting the highest engagement, reach, and impact, alongside high levels of consumer trust.

Realtors can optimize their TV campaigns by complementing them online – a strategy that has a lasting impact. TV shows/advertising and digital video are hot media options at the current time. It is worth considering a cross-platform approach, where those who can apply the learnings from television to digital video and vice versa will be the ultimate winners.

Video and Social Media

The TV show and/or commercial can be put to video through YouTube and social media links such as Facebook, LinkedIn, Google+, Twitter and others. This media draws the eye and attracts the 'click' action. You have the added benefit of posting the video to your homepage or a high traffic landing page—the likelihood that the viewer will stay on that page increases and they are likely to continue to click through your website. Link building and social shares should be a key part of your SEO strategy.

Planning and running video ads and social media promotion online prior to the TV show or ad campaign boosts brand recall for the TV show by 33%.

The different types of media, including print, radio, television and Internet, are in direct competition, but in certain cases, media convergence, collaboration advertising can give more credibility and have a huge overall impact to a realtor's marketing campaign.

Different types of advertising:

- *Print advertising:* Newspapers, magazines, brochures, flyers, direct mail.
- *Outdoor advertising:* Billboards, kiosks, trade-shows, bus shelters, bus and car wraps, shopping malls, community centers, and events.
- *Broadcast advertising:* Television, radio and the Internet.
- *Online advertising:* Pay per click, social network advertising, pop-up advertising.

Positive effects/advantages of social media advertising:

- Through these sites realtors can establish contact with entrepreneurs, corporate people, the general consumer and gain valuable information from them.
- Targets a wide audience, making it a useful and effective sales tool
- Facilitates open communication leading to discovery and delivery information
- Saves time and costs by providing faster communication

What type of media convergence or collaboration is feasible for a realtor's marketing campaign largely depends on individual marketing budgets. Careful consideration must be given to the chosen option/s to maximize exposure at minimum expense.

The best methods of media convergence is to promote your online network TV show in conjunction with radio broadcast, press releases, newspaper notifications, and photography with social media exposure.

Chapter 47: 115 steps to show value and get the contract!

Many home buyers and sellers are not aware of the true value that a realtor provides during the course of a real estate transaction.

At the same time, realtors have generally assumed that the professional knowledge and just plain hard work that go into bringing about a successful transaction is widely known, understood and appreciated by the general public—but that is not always the case.

Realtors often overlook the necessary step of providing the buyer/seller with a complete list of real estate tasks performed mostly behind the scenes by admin staff, outsourced, organized, implemented and completed by the realtor and/ or team.

When these tasks are outlined in a pre-listing package or on the actual listing presentation or buyer's appointment, they will in turn always guarantee that the buyer/seller will see the utmost value in your business and further assist you in finalizing the contract.

For most full-service real estate agents, when you list your home or sign a buyer's agency with them, they receive no compensation unless and until the sale closes.

By contrast, there are firms that offer reduced rates for limited services in exchange for an up-front flat fee, with the seller bearing full responsibility for all the other steps and procedures in the selling process. In short, this is not professional as you can see the number of tasks that are important to a transaction and, believe me, there are more. In actuality, the old saying stands true, "You typically always get what you pay for."

There are over a hundred typical actions, research steps, procedures, processes and review stages in a successful residential real estate transaction that are normally provided by full service, full time real estate agents/brokerages in return for the real estate fees.

Depending on the transaction, some may take minutes, hours, or even days to complete. More importantly, they represent the level of skill, knowledge and attention to detail required along with having help and guidance from someone who fully understands the process.

There are innumerable 'tasks' that a realtor provides for you. Here are just 115 of them!

Pre-Listing Activities:

1. Make appointment with seller for listing presentation.

2. Send seller a written or e-mail confirmation of listing appointment and call to confirm.

3. Research all comparable currently listed properties.

4. Research sales activity for past 6 months to a year through databases.

5. Research "Average Days on Market" for this property type, price range and location.

6. Download and review property tax roll information.

7. Prepare "Comparable Market Analysis" (CMA) to establish fair market value.

8. Research property's ownership and deed type.

9. Research property's public record information for lot size and dimensions.

10. Research and verify legal description.

11. Research property's current use and zoning.

12. Verify legal names of owner(s) in public property records.

13. Prepare listing presentation package with above materials.

14. Perform exterior Curb Appeal Assessment of subject property.

15. Confirm current public schools and explain impact of schools on market value.

Listing Appointment Presentation:

16. Give seller an overview of current market conditions and projections.

17. Review agent's credentials and accomplishments in the market.

18. Present company's profile and position in the marketplace.

19. Present 'CMA Results to Seller,' including Comparables, Solds, Current Listings and Expireds.

20. Offer pricing strategy based on current market conditions.

21. Discuss goals with seller to market effectively.

22. Explain market power and benefits of Multiple Listing Service.

23. Explain web marketing, Internet Data Display and Social Media.

24. Explain the work the brokerage and agent do behind the scenes

25. Explain agent's role in taking calls to screen for qualified buyers.

26. Review and explain all clauses in Listing Contract and obtain seller's signature.

Once Property is Under Listing Agreement:

27. Measure overall, interior room sizes and square footage.

28. Confirm lot size with owners copy of survey, if available.

29. Obtain house plans, if applicable and available.

30. Review house plans and make copy.

31. Prepare showing instructions and showing time window with seller.

32. Verify current loan information with owner and lender(s).

33. Check assumability of loan(s) and any special requirements.

34. Discuss possible buyer financing alternatives and options with seller.

35. Review current appraisal if available.

36. Calculate average utility usage from last 12 months of bills.

37. Research and verify city sewer/septic tank system.

38. Water System: Calculate average water fees or rates from last 12 months of bills.

39. Well water: Confirm well status, depth and output from Well Report.

40. Natural gas: Research/verify availability and supplier's name and telephone number.

41. Verify security system, current term of service and whether owned or leased.

42. Compile list of completed repairs and maintenance items.

43. Have extra key made for lockbox.

44. Verify if property has rental units involved. If so, verify all rents.

45. Inform tenants of listing and discuss how showings will be handled.

46. Arrange for installation of yard sign(s).

47. Review results of Curb Appeal Assessment with seller to improve salability.

48. Review results of Interior Décor Assessment, staging and décor.

49. Load listing into Realtor software program and upload to MLS.

Entering Property in Multiple Listing Service Database:

50. Prepare MLS Profile Sheet - Realtor is responsible for quality and accuracy of listing data.

51. Proofread MLS database listing for accuracy - including proper placement in mapping function.

52. Add property to company's Active Listings list.

53. Provide seller with signed copies of Listing Agreement and MLS Profile Sheet Data Form within 48 hours.

54. Take additional photos for upload into MLS and use in flyers. Discuss efficacy of panoramic/virtual tour photography.

Marketing The Listing:

55. Create print and Internet ads with seller's input.

56. Coordinate showings with owners, tenants, and other realtors. Return all calls - weekends included.

57. Install electronic lockbox if authorized by owner.

58. Prepare mailing and contact list.

59. Generate mail—merge letters to contact list.

60. Order and prepare flyers "Just Listed" labels and reports.

61. Review comparable MLS listings regularly to ensure property remains competitive in price, terms, conditions and availability.

62. Prepare property marketing brochure for open houses and seller's review.

63. Arrange for printing or copying of supply of marketing brochures or flyers.

64. Place marketing brochures in all company agent mail boxes.

65. Mail Out "Just Listed" notice to all neighbourhood residents.

66. Provide marketing data to buyers coming through international relocation networks.

67. Price changes sent promptly to all Internet groups.

68. Reprint/supply brochures promptly as needed.

69. Feedback e-mails sent to buyers' agents after showings.

70. Review weekly Market Study.

71. Discuss lockbox showing reports and feedback from showing agents with seller to determine if changes will accelerate the sale.

72. Place regular weekly update calls to seller to discuss marketing and pricing.

73. Promptly enter price changes in MLS listing database.

The Offer and Contract:

74. Receive and review all 'Offer to Purchase' contracts submitted by buyers or buyers' agents.

75. Evaluate offer(s) and prepare a "net sheet" on each for the owner for comparison purposes.

76. Counsel seller on offers. Explain merits and weakness of each component of each offer.

77. Contact buyers' agents to review buyer's qualifications and discuss offer.

78. Confirm buyer is pre-qualified by calling loan officer.

79. Obtain pre-qualification letter on buyer from loan officer.

80. Negotiate all offers on seller's behalf, setting time limit for loan approval and closing date.

81. Prepare and convey any counter offers, acceptance or amendments to buyer's agent.

82. Email or Fax copies of contract and all addendums to closing attorney or title company.

83. When 'Offer to Purchase Contract' is accepted and signed by seller, deliver to buyer's agent.

84. Record and promptly deposit buyer's deposit money in broker's trust account.

85. Deliver copies of fully signed Offer to Purchase contract to seller.

86. Email/Fax/deliver copies of Offer to Purchase contract to Selling Agent.

87. Email/Fax/deliver copies of Offer to Purchase contract to lender.

88. Provide copies of signed Offer to Purchase contract for office file.

89. Advise seller in handling additional Offers to Purchase submitted between sold conditional and sold firm.

90. Change status in MLS to "Sold conditional or awaiting deposit cheque."

91. Review tenant's credit report results—if it is a rental transaction—advise seller.

92. Assist buyer with obtaining financing, if applicable and follow-up as necessary.

93. Relay final approval of buyer's loan application to seller.

Home Inspection:

94. Coordinate buyer's professional home inspection with seller.

95. Assist and accompany buyer to home inspection and negotiate any problems and remedies as a result of the home inspection.

96. Review home inspector's report.

97. Enter completion into transaction management tracking software program.

98. Ensure seller's compliance with Home Inspection clause requirements.

99. Recommend or assist seller with identifying and negotiating with contractors to perform any required repairs.

100. Negotiate payment of all required repairs on seller's behalf, if needed.

Closing Preparations and Duties:

101. Contract is signed by all parties.

102. Coordinate closing process with buyer's agent and lender.

103. Update closing forms and files.

104. Ensure all parties have all forms and information needed to close the sale.

105. Co-ordinate with lawyer and keep updated.

106. Assist in solving any title problems (boundary disputes, easements, etc.)

107. Work with buyer's agent to schedule/conduct buyer's final walk-through prior to closing.

108. Review documents with closing agent (attorney).

109. Provide earnest money deposit check from trust account to closing agent.

110. Coordinate this closing with seller's next purchase and resolve any timing problems.

111. Refer sellers to a realtor at their destination, if applicable.

112. Change MLS status to 'Sold.' Enter sale date, price, selling broker, etc.

113. Close out listing in transaction management program.

Follow Up After Closing:

114. Attempt to clarify and resolve any conflicts about repairs if buyer is not satisfied.

115. Respond to any follow-up calls and provide any additional information required from office files.

Chapter 48: Handling objections in real estate sales

Objections are often the way clients gather additional information or clarification on something they don't understand. Try to see objections as opportunities! In most cases, objections simply pinpoint a client's major concerns or key areas of interest.

If you get defensive or take the objection personally, you immediately lose any chance to influence the decision making and the opportunity to make the sale. Don't forget—an objection is better than an outright "no" because it gives you a place to begin or continue the conversation. Here are some key strategies and logistical ways to handle objections:

- *Acknowledge the objection:* You should be happy the client has expressed their objection. In many cases clients never voice them but merely walk away. Don't try to resolve the objection immediately. Always thank your customer when they put an objection before you. I can't tell you the number of times a simple thank you has helped to diffuse a situation. If the objection becomes emotional, don't try to use logic. You need to deal with the client's feelings first.

- *Empathize. Feeling first:* Although scripting is an important part of every salesperson's repertoire, what you need to say next, following an objection, should ideally come from the heart, not a book. After thanking the customer for bringing the objection to your attention, empathize in a way that will help further diffuse the situation. For example: That is an excellent point you raised and I can see your concern. Tell me more... or I'm sorry you feel that way, I hear what you're saying and I think I can help... By speaking from the heart, the customer is more likely to open up and share with you their concerns and feelings.

- *Clarify. Let the discovery begin:* Once you have taken care of the clients' feelings, you need clarification about the issue/s of concern and what it means to the client. Good customer discovery always focuses on asking open-ended questions. If you get stuck, just do what every 4-year-old does and ask "why?", you'll be amazed at how powerful that little question can be! Building rapport (See Chapter 42: Build connections—create instant rapport) is equally important during the discovery phase. Experts say it takes 4-5 layers of questions to truly uncover the nature of the objection. Finally, restate what you heard in your own words and ask them to confirm that you've correctly understood their reasoning behind the objection.

- *Recommendations:* Showing them value! They must see the value in you, your service and what your offering. They must feel confident that you understand and can fulfill their needs. Be sure to back it up with proof and customer references. Once you have made the recommendations, pause... Don't jump right in and see if it's okay. Don't second guess yourself before the client has had time to mull it over. You may need to probe further till you uncover all objections before you can thank them for making the choice to work with you. Remember, managing objections requires practice but if you take these four rules and apply them to your business. You'll see very quickly that they do work!

Most Common Real Estate Objections and Scripts

When you learn to understand and effectively handle objections, you will be able to close more appointments. A great way to achieve this is to develop answers (script them) to common objections. The answers should be short, precise and to the point.

Here are some common real estate objections, and scripts that I recommend you use to overcome them, to convert more new clients. Practice these scripts daily, adjust them to your own words and style of talking.

- *Objection #1: "I have a friend in the business."* Your answer: "Mr. Seller, almost everyone knows someone who has a real estate license these days. If he is as good a friend as you say, I'm sure he wants what is best for you correct? (Yes?) Great! When do you plan on interviewing your friend and seeing exactly what he can do in terms of marketing? (Tomorrow at 5?) Wonderful. Let's do this—why don't I come over tomorrow at 6 and show you what I have to offer and that way you will be able to make a fully informed decision as to what is best for YOU. Does that sound reasonable?"
  or
  Your answer: "Are you looking to get your home sold or are you trying to help your friend out? My concern is this: did you know that 10% of the agents do 90% of the business; is your friend part of the 10%? And if he is not, are you willing to risk your friendship if things don't go well?"

- *Objection #2: "We would like to think about it."* Your answer: "I understand completely, Ms. Seller. A decision like this needs some time to think over. And what I would like to recommend is that I give you a call next week to get your thoughts and to determine the next steps. How does Wednesday at 6:15 look on your calendar?"
  or
  Your answer: "I understand completely. If I were sitting where you are now

I'd probably want to think about it too. If I may ask, one quick question: "what concerns do you still have?"
or
"what is causing you to hesitate?"
or
"what is your number one concern about not proceeding further?"
or
"what will your final decision be based upon?"
This type of probing gets the prospect to open up and help you determine if the objection is real or otherwise. If the probing didn't help:
Your answer: "Fair enough. But John, we've spent a bit of time reviewing your situation and there seems to be a good fit. Please level with me, 'What's holding you back?'"

- *Objection #3: "I want to find a house before I put mine on the market."* Your answer: "I understand your concern about your new home. I've brought you a list of current listings that fit your need. Check these out and we will start looking. Once this house goes under contract, we will put an offer on your #1 choice. We'll move to close both homes on the same day, which means one move for you! You are in good hands. I will take care of you."
or
Your answer: "I agree, finding your new home is important and the unfortunate thing is it may take a month or more for your home to sell. Then it will take another 3-4 months to close and, by that time, any home that you could have found would already have been sold. Let's get to work on getting your home sold, so you don't have to wait any longer than is necessary to get moved into your new home. Sound good?"

- *Objection #4: "I'm not ready yet. I want to fix a few things first."* You answer: "If you do not mind, I would like to review your list with you. Just to make sure the items you are doing will 'help' the sale of your home and be worth your investment. Would you have time to meet tomorrow afternoon or evening?"

- *Objection #5: "I am going to talk with other realtors."* You answer: "That's fine. Help me understand. What is it that other realtors will provide you that we have not discussed?" (seller response) "Would tomorrow morning work for us to review the differences between my plan to sell your home and my competitor's ideas?"

- *Objection #6: "I am going to try to sell it myself."* You answer: "I am just curious, how do you plan on marketing your home?" or "...representing the buyer?" "...responding to buyer leads?" "...being available for buyer showings?" (seller response) "If I had a proven plan for selling your home at top market value, would you be interested in hearing it?"

- Objection #7: *"We are going to relist with the same realtor."* Your answer: You are thinking about relisting with the same realtor? I understand. Thanks for sharing that with me. Can I make a suggestion? Right now you feel that the same realtor is your best bet, right? Would you like to be certain? I'm merely suggesting a second opinion. Does that make sense? Can I be that second opinion?"

- Objection #8: *"We are not ready to sell yet. We would like to wait."* Your answer: "Thanks for sharing that with me. I really appreciate it. (Build a bridge.) Do you mind if I ask you a question? If you had an offer on your home in the next 30 days for the right price and the right closing date, would you consider it? (I might) If you can give me 15 minutes of your time, I can let you know if I can do that."

- Objection #9: *"We have to sell our house first."* For Buyers - Your answer: "I understand...that's the general idea. Would it help to know how much you could sell your current home for while we are still looking around for your new home? When would you like to move into your new home? Would you like to make an appointment for a market evaluation?"
  Or for buyer:
  "Have you met with a lender to see if you qualify to buy a new home before you sell? Or do you need to sell your current home first?"

- Objection #10: *"We are looking for a relative/friend."* For Buyers - Your answer: "Would it help if I set your relative/friend up on a search so he/she could see all of the homes for sale that fit his/her criteria online first? That way you guys could just contact me when you want to see the inside of one? Great, what is your relative/friend looking for? What is their contact number and email?"

- Objection #11: *"We are going to wait. We aren't ready now."* For Buyer/Seller - Your answer: "Understood. There is a lot to do before buying a new home: preparing your current home for sale, meeting with a lender, insurance, inspectors, repairs, finding a home, etc. Would you like some help with all of that?"

Chapter 49: Geographical farming—the next step up!

Geographical farming is essentially about becoming the neighbourhood real estate specialist in the community. The concept is pivotal to establish your reputation as the area expert. It is important to outperform the competition and know the area better than anyone. You must consistently supply clients with neighbourhood real estate information and relevant statistics. You have to develop a relationship with the residents of the neighbourhood so they will choose YOU over the competition.

Farming takes time and with the number of real estate agents out there competing against you, it can be costly to establish yourself. Be prepared to make it a long term investment. Consistency is the king of farming!

Farming has these great advantages:

- Developing long-term relationships with your customers and other businesses within the area—oftentimes this is the greatest reward.

- Having the satisfaction of customer loyalty and referral support. The longer you service the community, the more recognition you will gain to the point of becoming a household name.

- Effective branding strategy as farming ensures your name comes up as the primary community real estate resource. It is a great long term marketing strategy.

The more you know about your neighbourhood, the better your edge. Farming can generate amazing results! Imagine seeing your real estate yard signs on every other block. Or being invited to every neighbourhood street party because the neighbours know and like you.

How do you choose a geographical farm area?
- *Determine what is the turnover rate in the area you are considering.* Find neighbourhoods with exceptional turnover (typically ranging from 5-10%) that will help you find where homes are selling in quantity, within the shortest amount of time and with the highest return. Usually 8% minimum turnover rate is ideal for a 'farm' area. If it is less than that, it will be unlikely you will be able to generate the business or sales to make it a useful 'farming' area.

- *How long have the occupants lived in their homes?* If a good number of homeowners have lived in the area from about three to six years, this could be an excellent opportunity to catch these homeowners before their next transition. Statistically, homeowners relocate every five years, giving you nearly ready-to-move customers.

- *What is the percentage of renters versus homeowners in the neighbourhood?* If there is a high percentage of renters, this may be an area to work with first-time buyers and renters moving into home ownership. Typically, this area would not be suitable for farming listings.

- *What is the price point or average sale?* There is a 'sweet spot' in every area – either the price point at which most of the homes sell or where the price demand is highest. As we consider these variables, we look for consistency in the number of homes for sale and their turnover.

- *Who are the dominant agents in the area?* The current competition in your chosen community is always important to assess–check whether a community has one or more dominant agents in the area and what is their percentage market share.

- *What is your farming budget?* Geographic farming is NOT a magic bullet, so ensure that the number of homes you are targeting matches your budget. Growing within your budget is the most successful approach. As you sell, you can invest a portion of the profit towards growing your farm.

- *Are you compatible with the area?* Now that you've found one or more communities that look good on paper, take stock of and be aware of local market trends, amenities, and share a common connection with local homeowners. Remember whichever farm you choose, you MUST want to sell the community as much as the homes themselves.

Real estate marketing and farming ideas

- neighbourhood market updates/newsletters

- 'just listed' and 'just sold' flyers

- telephone calls/introduction to neighbours

- door knocking

- private for sales/expired

- open house events

- community parties

- neighbourhood websites

- email campaigns

- social media/Facebook

Plant and nurture your seeds –

- Develop your marketing plan for the target 'farm' area and include your contact messages. Plan your campaign for the full year.

- Start by finding out what your customers want and need.

- Ask questions in the neighbourhood. Find a way to fulfill those needs or provide resources that do.

- Contact your 'farm' a minimum of once per month by mailer. If you can afford to, consider contacting your farm 2-3 times per month for the first six months to a year and then you can reduce it down to at least once per month.

- In between these times, touch or contact your farm once or twice a month by phone, in person, through open houses, by email or through social media.

- Develop a newsletter for the community both online and off. Use your website to provide neighbourhood information as well as home delivery.

- Find local vendors that service garage doors, landscaping, deck repair, bug and rodent removal, roof repair, etc. Become the local referral expert for home repairs.

- Offer ideas for home improvement, better curb appeal, etc. Offer ideas about anything that will make the neighbourhood a better place to live.

- Giveaways—Magnetic marketing tools – calendars, sports schedules, notepads, tips and hints, gifts and gadgets for the home, flashlight, and numerous other ideas.

- Find local activities to sponsor – fundraising, school activities, senior meal delivery, BBQ's, Fall Fairs, etc.

- Work with a local business who is willing to offer a discount on an item for you to advertise their business in your newsletter. For example, restaurant certificate, free ice cream cone with the coupon from your mailer or website.

- Develop a home buyer's or home seller's seminar and hold it at your local library or recreation center.

There are tons of ideas to benefit your geo-farm area. (Check other chapters in this book). Rent your local community centre for 'Swim and Skate' days. Rent your local theatre for movie days. Rent an ice cream truck, give away pumpkins, organize a children's colouring contest, Christmas parties and the list goes on. These activities keep your name in the customer's minds, so when they go to sell their home—who do you think they may consider? Who will seem like a friend because of their long time association with the neighbourhood? Well of course...You! You are seen as 'The Realtor Specialist' who has spent a great deal of time working in the community, giving back to the residents and providing the best service, backed by area experience. Who will they call first, the person who sends them the most information and is selling the most homes in the neighbourhood?

Do take your business to the next level—consider Geographical Farming! Plant the seed! Reap the harvest!

Chapter 50: Power thoughts for realtors

To be successful in real estate, you must always and consistently put your clients' best interests first. When you do, your personal needs will be realized beyond our expectations.

Read these power thoughts daily. Use when necessary to inspire and motivate you, to offer you guidance, strengthen your spirit, help you accomplish and succeed in your goals or just simply use to brighten your day or someone else's!

Power thoughts

- Don't give up! Don't take anything personally! Don't take no for an answer.

- Always look at the big picture. Don't let the little things in life and business affect you or bring you down.

- Keep the big vision in sight. Fuel your vision with perseverance.

- Conquer the addiction to distraction—and overcome the urge of procrastination.

- Focus is as important as intelligence—Intelligence = Focus, discipline and determination.

- Don't dilute your *Focus* because it dilutes your *Energy*.

- Stop auto-excusing and deliver results as efficiently as possible.

- Leave people better than you find them. Inspire them to do good.

- Be so good at what you do that people seek you as a mentor, role model, coach or Go-To professional.

- The moment people start to tear you down means that you have made an impact.—Think about it!

- Who do you want to become? What difference do you make in your world? Whatever dream you have, magnify the dream 10 times and go for it!

- Be creative and allow yourself the freedom to follow your creative talents, interests and passions. Be ready to take risks. Love what you do!

- Don't censor or deny yourself quiet time, creative time or fun time.

- Think outside the box. You will be innovative, show initiative, and be much more interesting company!

- Surround yourself with the best kind of people. Stay away from toxic, negative, low energy people who will draw you down.

- Negativity can be contagious! Keep that smile on your face no matter how your day is going. Don't gossip or be drawn into it.

- Get a mentor/s. Surround yourself with a group of people who inspire you. Networking opens up your social circle, but be careful who you allow in as 'keepers.'

- Learn something new every day. Be open and listen to ideas and opinions. Give advice when asked, even with clients, but hold your peace if you encounter differing views that do not sway you.

- Remember you don't have to *win* every battle. Sometimes it makes sense to just stay quiet.

- Learn from the experience of successful agents. Adapt their strategies where appropriate.

- Evaluate all pertinent ideas, but implement only the best ones that feel true to you.

- The will to win must include the will to prepare. Good results require the necessary prep work to be put in.

- Motivation will get you started. Habit will keep you going.

- Surround yourself with great people—and build your team slowly. There is value in expansion and rounding out the expertise and skill set.

- Be a mentor or coach to someone! The feeling is unbelievable! A mentor empowers a person to see a bright future and to believe it can be attained.

- Be a leader! Leadership is about Inspiration, Influence and Impact. It shows you have 'arrived' at your goals and are now giving back to your industry.

- Ask yourself everyday: how may I help the most people possible? How may I best serve people and understand their needs?

- Practice random acts of kindness. A simple act of kindness can make a tremendous impact on the receiving person's life and it will be reciprocated beyond your expectations. It is called Karma—believe it and pass it on.

THE LAST WORD ...

Congratulations! Good work! You have finished the book! You have covered a great deal of material on real estate and beyond. Now, your challenge is to implement these new strategies, bring results and lasting changes to your life and your business.

We encourage you to take the first step. From there, those unexpected wins will motivate you to try out more and more lessons in this book as you win more challenges, reach your life goals, either by accomplishing the purchase of your first home, increasing your investment portfolio, flipping and renovating houses or adding more systems to improve your business and generate income.

The major solution in this book is to learn how to gain control over your thoughts and the ability to choose how you react to situations. You have the power to choose what you want out of life. So when you make powerful requests of yourself and decide, be ready to accept whatever comes—both the good and unusual. Remember nothing happens overnight and persistence is the key. Keep your focus. Believe in your dreams and the results that can take you to the next level!

When I decided to write this book, I really had no idea how much work and time was involved. I had a major deadline and unexpected time commitment. Still, I had a vision, a message that I was passionate about and I had a deep devotion to share it. With persistence and focus, in my hectic life as a realtor, I plodded on with purpose, as it created an environment of growth and expansion and more opportunities unfolded for me in a new and exciting way that I never imagined.

I encourage you to do the same. Live your dream. Show compassion. Follow your heart. Create your own happiness. Enjoy the little things in life. Laugh out loud. Make a wish. Be your best self. Cherish every moment. Dream big. Believe in miracles. Embrace every possibility and remember to breathe... I hope you enjoyed reading this book as much as I enjoyed writing it! Find your magic (passion) in life and your dreams will come true. Success is unlimited. It's up to you!

ABOUT THE AUTHOR

Carmela Zita Kapeleris

Carmela Zita Kapeleris was born in Canada to Italian immigrant parents. She lives in Mississauga with her husband and two adult children, both of whom encouraged her to pursue her talents and write this book.

Carmela has inspired and empowered hundreds of people into a life of personal and business fulfillment through her various speaking engagements, workshops, multimedia and philanthropic platforms. She is the host/producer of Kapeleris Talk TV–Real Estate & Beyond that promotes business, wealth and healthy living.

She has a passion for helping people find their dream home and is an award winning Broker Realtor with over 30 years' experience in the industry. She is known to belong to one of the top sales teams in Canada. She is the recipient of many awards including the Hall of Fame-2005, Lifetime Achievement-2010 and Service Excellence. She has international sales status working on projects in Florida, Mexico, Dominican Republic, and Costa Rica. She has facilitated workshops in Vancouver, Calgary, Ontario, and the U.S. She and her partner/ husband have been keynote real estate speakers in Europe.

Carmela is the founder of a non-profit networking organization and 'woman helping women' group. She is a proud advocate for World Vision, Children's Miracle Network, Breast Cancer Awareness and Adopt a Senior. She has been featured on radio, TV, newspapers and Profiles of Success Magazine, RESAAS and other publications.

She was recently named by the City Mayor as "an icon in her Community" and dubbed by her colleagues as one of the most innovative, collaborative thinkers in our time, creating a culture of leadership excellence. Carmela is truly energetic and passionate in her delivery of this book, leaving a distinct impression in the real estate industry and unique mark in this world.

The author may be contacted for speaking engagements and workshops at info@kapeleris.com or ckapeleristeam@gmail.com. Website: www.kapeleris.com

"90% of all millionaires become so through owning real estate. More money has been made in real estate than in all industrial investments combined. The wise young man or wage earner of today invests his money in real estate."

– Andrew Carnegie

www.ingramcontent.com/pod-product-compliance
Lightning Source LLC
Chambersburg PA
CBHW061021220326
41597CB00017BB/2243